LIEUTENANT-COLONEL

JOHN HAUGHTON

Commandant of the 36th Sikhs

A HERO OF TIRAH

LIEUTENANT-COLONEL

JOHN HAUGHTON

Commandant of the 36th Sikhs

A HERO OF TIRAH

A Memoir

BY

MAJOR A. C. YATE

GYAN

Published by

GYAN

Gyan Publishing House
5, Ansari Road
Daryaganj, New Delhi-110002
Phone: 011-47034999, 9811692060
E-mail: books@gyanbooks.com

Distribution Network
gyanbooks.com
India, USA, Canada, UK, Australia

ISBN:978-81-212-4934-8 (HB)
First Published, 1900

2nd Impression 2024

Printed at: Gyan Press, Delhi.

LIEUTENANT-COLONEL JOHN HAUGHTON COMMANDANT OF THE 36TH SIKHS A HERO OF TIRAH

Author: MAJOR A. C. YATE

LIEUTENANT-COLONEL

JOHN HAUGHTON

Lieut-Colonel John Haughton.

Commandant of the 36th Sikhs.

LIEUTENANT-COLONEL
JOHN HAUGHTON

Commandant of the 36th Sikhs

A HERO OF TIRAH

A Memoir

BY

MAJOR A. C. YATE

2ND (DUKE OF CONNAUGHT'S OWN) BALUCH BATTALION

F.R.G.S.

AUTHOR OF "ENGLAND AND RUSSIA FACE TO FACE IN ASIA,"

ETC.

"In all retirements he stuck doggedly to the rear-guard until he saw the last of his column safely out of danger."

"LUMSDEN OF THE GUIDES," p. 120.

LONDON

JOHN MURRAY, ALBEMARLE STREET

1900

SHREWSBURY SCHOOL.

Founded 1551.

UPPINGHAM SCHOOL.

Founded 1584.

THIS MEMOIR IS, BY PERMISSION,

Dedicated

TO THE

HEAD-MASTERS

OF

SHREWSBURY AND UPPINGHAM SCHOOLS,

AT WHICH GENERAL JOHN COLPOYS HAUGHTON

AND LIEUT.-COLONEL JOHN HAUGHTON

WERE RESPECTIVELY

EDUCATED.

PREFACE.

In these days, when reviewers ring out their clang of warning against the flood of memorial literature, to swell the current without a cause would be worse than waste. The waters must be waters of life, and the source must be pure, that those who drink thereof may profit thereby. Popularity is seductive, but not always a gauge of literary merit, gentle bearing, or good taste. It is these alone that bear the test of time; and it is on time that we may rely to show (for instance) that "Tom Brown's Schooldays," and not "Stalky & Co.," portrays the characters, the principles, and the manners which we desire as examples for our boys.

During the War in South Africa, some of our best-known military critics, and notably Mr. Spenser Wilkinson, have dwelt on the fact that the average British officer is in no sense a serious student of his profession. It is possible that the Memoir may appeal to that officer in a way that the Manual apparently does not do. It is essential that the examples of our best soldiers should be set before the Army—not only of those who have attained high rank and held onerous commands, but also of those who have distinguished themselves in less prominent capacities. It is the many juniors who, under the few Generals, win our battles. It is said that the non-commissioned officers are the backbone of the battalion. I venture, then, to say that the Commanding Officer stiffens that backbone. The "selection" of a Commanding Officer is a matter of the first importance; and all those who take a thorough interest in the Army must always devoutly pray for the guidance of those in whose hands "selection" lies, and for their delivery from the many temptations that beset "selection."

When we do find a Commanding Officer who has risen to that post, without favour or affection, who in that post has won the more than regard and respect of those under him, and who has personified a very high ideal of coolness, capacity for command, courage, and devotion, the example of that man ought not to be lost to Her Majesty's Army. It is one that every soldier may do well to know and follow, and it is one that every parent may set before a soldier son. On Lieut.-Colonel John Haughton the mantle of his father had fallen. Both father and son were, in every sense of the word, gallant and good men. Yet to-day Lieutenant John Colpoys Haughton, the staunch defender of Charikar in 1841, is known but to the few serious students of Indian Frontier warfare; while, to my knowledge, the name of Lieut.-Colonel John Haughton is, within three years of his noble death at Shinkamar, "caviare to the general," which, being interpreted, is "a dead letter to the man in the street." Nevertheless, the name of John Haughton is worthy to stand by that of John Nicholson, as one who gave himself without stint for his country and for his brethren-in-arms. The two men present strong points of resemblance, in their fine physique, in their great influence over natives, in their grand moral qualities, and in their fearlessness of danger.

My chief and best fellow-worker in writing this Memoir has been Colonel Haughton's widow. I am also indebted for information and help to Mrs. J. C. Haughton, and Mrs. Richard Haughton, Colonel C. H. Palmer, Lieut.-General Sir G. B. Wolseley, Major Gunning Hunter of the 10th "Jats," and to several other officers who prefer to be incogniti; also to several of the Masters and old boys of Uppingham School.

The conviction, confirmed if not engendered by Dr. Warre's lecture at the Royal United Service Institution on the 27th June last, of the very important part that Public Schools might, nay, ought to take in the military training of the youth of the upper and middle classes of the Nation, made me desirous of associating this book with the two Public Schools, Shrewsbury and Uppingham, at which General J. C. Haughton and his son had been respectively educated. The courtesy and kindness of the Head-masters of those Schools, the Rev. Prebendary H. W. Moss and the Rev. E. C. Selwyn, B.D., have enabled me to gratify this wish. Sir Philip Sidney and Sir Claude MacDonald—the one the *preux chevalier* of his period, and the first and foremost of the soldiers educated at Shrewsbury, the other the staunch defender of the British Legation at Peking, and the most distinguished of the recent accessions to the Honour-Roll of Uppingham—are, so to speak, the first and last links in a chain that unites the earlier years of our great Queen Elizabeth with the later years of our still greater Queen Victoria. A Public School and its *alumni* possess a reciprocal power of action and reaction, which is the mainspring of the great influence that Public Schools exercise on the manhood of the Nation. I am proud to acknowledge the debt I owe to Shrewsbury.

In addition to private sources of information, I have, by the courtesy of the Editor, made use of the special correspondence in the *Times of India* from September, 1897, to February, 1898. I have also consulted the books published by Captain Shadwell, Colonel Hutchinson, and Mr. Lionel James, and by the *Pioneer* and *Civil and Military Gazette* Presses. I am indebted to the Rev. Father Mansfield, Roman Catholic chaplain at Peshawar, for the photograph of the grave and monument in the cemetery there, and to the Rev. G. H. Mullins for that of the memorial tablet placed by the 35th and 36th Sikhs in Uppingham School Chapel. Some of the smaller illustrations are from photographs taken by Colonel Haughton himself. For others I am indebted to Messrs. Law Brothers of Ambala, Dr. A. H. Brown of Amritsar, and one or two other persons. Good photographs of scenes in Tirah I have found difficult to procure. The map of Tirah is based on the best authorities available.

In the Introduction and in Chapters I. and II. I have sought to show the sources from which Lieut.-Colonel John Haughton derived or inherited the high qualities of military leadership that he displayed in Tirah, at the same time giving an account of his ancestry, and of his father's distinguished career. In Chapters III., IV., and V. I have dealt with his early days, and with the first twenty-five years of his service, from 1872 to 1897. In Chapters VI. to XI. I have related the deeds that won him fame.

The last Chapter is a *résumé* of ideas suggested by recent warfare and the condition of the British Army. Appendix A gives Colonel Haughton's impressions of the Tirah campaign, written while every event was fresh in his mind, and just a fortnight before his death.

As regards Oriental names, I have adopted that spelling which I considered would be understood by all. When I quote other persons' writings, I do not alter their spelling of names.

A. C. YATE.

WOODHILL PLACE, BATH,
September 2, 1900.

CONTENTS.

LIST OF ILLUSTRATIONS.

MAPS.

LIEUTENANT-COLONEL

JOHN HAUGHTON.

INTRODUCTION.

PART I.

"The right faith of man is not intended to give him repose, but to enable him to do his work. It is not intended that he should look away from the place he lives in now, and cheer himself with thoughts of the place he is to live in next, but that he should look straight into this world, in faith that if he does his work thoroughly here, some good to others or himself, with which, however, he is not at present concerned, will come of it hereafter."—AUTHOR UNKNOWN.

WHILE engaged, eighteen months ago, in collecting and studying the material for a memoir of Lieut.-Colonel John Haughton, I for the first time read with due attention the defence of Charikar in November, 1841. I had been inquiring in my own mind whence Colonel Haughton had derived the inborn qualities which won for him fame. I knew that he had seen no active service before Tirah; and yet, amid a host of frontier officers of long experience, he stood forth conspicuous as the man who knew how to foil the Afridis at their own game. After reading the story of his father's defence of Charikar, I felt that the secret was revealed. It was a case of hereditary intuition. The following extract from a letter written to me by Colonel C. H. Palmer in the autumn of 1899, independently confirms this view:—

"Again you put it to me—how John Haughton learnt to fight the frontier tribesmen. I cannot really tell you. He certainly could not have learnt it with us, for we saw no service while he was with us; but (this is only *my* way of accounting for it) Jack was a soldier born, he was always reading useful accounts of campaigns, and I expect his father told him much of his experiences; and further, I think there is a sort of 'instinct' in *some* men, as well as in mere animals, beyond the ordinary, or rather extraordinary human knowledge, which makes one man '*all there*' under certain circumstances, where another man of apparently equal mental calibre is an utter failure, and worse than useless (*i.e.* like a dead man in a boat), and I think Jack had this instinct; and further, Jack so thoroughly knew and studied the characters of all natives he came in contact with, and when you really *know* one native, or at any rate several of different castes and 'jats,'* you can pretty well know what they will be likely to do in certain circumstances on service or otherwise. This, as I say again, is only *my* way of accounting for Jack's being such a glorious success at the 'first time of asking,' for it was his first active service, and I feel sure he would have been just as great a success against any enemy, white or black, had his life been spared."

A year ago, the Memoir of "Lumsden of the Guides" came into my hands. I read there of the Paladins of frontier warfare—Sir Colin Campbell,

* *I.e.* sorts.

Sir Sydney Cotton, Sir Harry Lumsden, Sir Neville Chamberlain, and others. One sentence that spoke volumes for Sir Colin Campbell (the General whom Lord Dalhousie constrained to resign his frontier command at Peshawar, and thus, unwittingly, paved for him a path to fame and a peerage) I determined to place on the title-page of this volume; for, if there was one guiding principle which Colonel Haughton exemplified, it was—Stand by the rearguard to the last. He proved his fidelity to it at Sarān-sar, at Tseri-Kandao, in the Dwatoi defile, and in the march down the Bāra Valley; and he sealed it with his blood at Shinkamar. It was his motto, and for that man can do no more than die, if fate so wills.

I could not mention here all the friends of Colonel Haughton whose sympathy and help and more than kindly letters have encouraged me to write this memoir. Some do not wish to be named. It was good to read those letters and realize how much a man and a soldier can make himself esteemed, respected, and beloved. There is in it a lesson not to be forgotten. Only one or two of these letters, and some extracts from others, can appear in this volume; but some of them will remain as an heirloom to be treasured by those to whom his memory is dearest. No man's life has been spent in vain who has inspired such friendship and such high esteem as Colonel Haughton did, and who has left such an example for those who come after him.

It is one of the kindly features of the usually sombre and often distasteful aspect of war, that it reveals such characters as his—men who stand a head and shoulders (I speak metaphorically, and not in allusion to Haughton's six feet six inches) above their fellow-men. It is refreshing to turn from bickering and recrimination—in which the Tirah expedition was too fruitful—to the study of a character which never stooped to the methods of meaner, though possibly, in the world's sight, more successful men.* Haughton never asked for anything. He was content to do his duty in that state in which it pleased superior authority to place him. In all his letters to his most intimate correspondent, his father, there is never a note of discontent. He was not a man of grievances. He did his work steadily and quietly, and one day, to his surprise and gratification, found he was appreciated. From that time (1885) his preferment was rapid. In nine years he rose from a wing officer to the command of a crack native regiment.

His existing letters to his father cover only the period from 1880 to September, 1887, when his father died. To him he could write on every Indian topic—his own career, the conditions of the

* The latter, as a rule, pass into oblivion, while the names of the nobler live. Many great Indian soldiers have been under the ban of superior authority. Henry Lawrence, Colin Campbell, Charles Napier, all incurred the displeasure of Lord Dalhousie. James Outram and Henry Durand were both under a cloud for a time. Havelock got little preferment, but lived long enough for deathless fame. Even John Nicholson was no favourite with John Lawrence. These are a few instances.

service, and every phase of official and political administration. With his father's death these letters cease. It is a remarkable thing, and indicative of the innate sympathy that existed between father and son, that the two wrote to each other as if they had lived together all their lives; the fact being that the son had scarcely seen his father at all. The most perfect confidence existed between them. Of his life in Russia, and while employed in the Intelligence Division of the War Office, and in the 35th and 36th Sikhs, we have little or no record from his own pen. It is not until the last six months of his life that his letters from the Samana Range and from Tirah recommence, to form a more or less connected narrative of what he did and what he thought. In his own letters and those of his relatives and friends exists a lasting testimony to his worth as a soldier, a gentleman, a husband, a son, and a friend. One brief quotation I will venture to make here. It is from a letter written to me in July, 1899, by Major Dillon, an officer who has himself won distinction in the frontier warfare of India. It ends with these words:

"All the officers in garrison, and they were many, attended his (Haughton's) funeral at Peshawar who could; for his name had become a talisman, and to many, as he was to myself, he was a dear personal friend. His name is still revered in his regiment, where he is talked about in the native ranks as something quite beyond the ordinary Sahib."

PART II.

In the simplest episodes of life the truth is a truant that almost defies search. In war it is either magnified by romance, or lost amid the confusion of conflict. The human senses unaided are but imperfect recorders of facts; and what they do record is distorted by personal predilection and bias. Science has introduced us to two forces, photography and electricity, which, when more fully developed, promise to supply the defects of the human senses, and which have no choice but to record the truth. Already the one reveals objects which the human eye is powerless to reflect; while by the other, sound and scene are recorded and reproduced. These two forces combined have now been adapted to the reproduction of every form of action and motion. It remains to utilize them to represent exactly the living scenes of war. We shall then know war as it is, not as the imaginations of war-artists depict it in our illustrated weeklies and on the walls of the Academy. Dargai inspired two paintings exhibited in 1898. Both were impossible. Photography, indeed, has given us true pictures of the scene of that action, though not of the action itself. Already that art reproduces for us many of the stiller scenes of a campaign. Instruments are only needed to recreate the stirring struggle of the battle-field, and even that has been done to some extent during the recent South African War. Till those instruments are perfected, human reason must endeavour to tone down the colouring of romance, and to sift truth from fiction. How hard that is, may be gathered from the controversial literature to which the Waterloo campaign has given rise. For instance, excellent evidence, including that of the Great Duke himself, can be adduced to show that Wellington *did* and *did not* ride over to Blucher's quarters at Wavre on the night of the 17th June. As for the far-famed order, "Up, Guards, and at them!" it has, long ago (together with Cambronne's "La Garde meurt mais ne se rend pas," Charles Napier's "Peccavi," and Sir George Pollock's "Advance Nott"), passed into the realm of myths,* whither it seems in time likely to be followed by the words which Colonel Mathias is said to have addressed to the Gordon Highlanders before the final assault on Dargai. Of five different accounts of that hard-fought action which have appeared in books alone, one does not mention the words at all, another reels out a long and impossible rigmarole, while the remaining three are far from agreeing as to the words used. And this within a few months of the event! † When we read the life

* *Pace* the *Times* (August 18, 1900), "the Duke's old saying about the Playing-Fields at Eton has" not yet "done its work." On the contrary, they and those of the other schools of England should furnish the primary instruction in that knowledge, the cultivation of which the Commander-in-Chief of the Army enjoined on the occasion of his visit to Aldershot.

† If we consider for one moment the conditions under which these words are said to have been spoken, we must realize that an authoritative record of them is scarcely possible. The gallantry of the

of such a soldier as Sir Charles MacGregor (twice wounded in the Mutiny, five times wounded and specially recommended for gallantry in China, twice wounded in Bhutan), and reflect that he never received the Victoria Cross, we begin to doubt whether that reward for bravery always goes to those who have best deserved it. At Colenso recently the curious distinction was drawn between the soldier who was brave "by order" and "without order." The courage of a Haughton was instinctive. The defence of Charikar by the young subaltern of twenty-four was a test of bravery and endurance with which no momentary flash of daring can compare; while the memory of John Haughton at Tseri Kandao, at Dwatoi, and at Shinkamar, will be handed down as a tradition of cool courage and steadfast valour. Neither father nor son, however, was decorated with the Victoria Cross.

It is more than probable that no critical history of the Tirah campaign will be published for another quarter of a century. The first volume of the first elaborated history of the Afghan War of 1878–81 has only recently appeared. This *fin-de-siècle* era abounds in histories and memoirs, Napoleonic, Crimean, Mutiny, etc. The middle of the twentieth century, when all eye-witnesses are numbered with the dead, though peradventure they may leave

Gordons and their Colonel on this memorable day needs no halo of sentiment, and history will not accept a mere fiction of journalism playing to the gallery. The words used can only be authenticated by him who spoke them and by those who heard them spoken, if indeed memory in such moments takes heed of words.

diaries and memoirs behind them, will probably produce the first history of the frontier fighting of 1897. It will then be a tangled web to unravel. Though, as I have mentioned, five narratives of the Tirah expedition have already appeared, none of them can claim the status of history; albeit, in years to come they will be the stand-by of the historian. They have told to Englishmen all the world over the unflinching gallantry and fortitude with which Her Majesty's troops, British and Native, carried out their duty from first to last throughout one of the most trying frontier campaigns that the army of India has ever faced. Severe weather, chilly marches and chillier bivouacs without tents and at times without food, reconnaissance, forage and convoy duties in an intricate country and along most difficult paths or tracks, and fighting at every step whether in advance or retreat,—these briefly summarize the chief features of a two months' campaign. The enemy never stood to fight, but harried our troops, day and night, on every possible opportunity. When the history of guerilla warfare is written, the Afridis will merit a prominent place in it. The record of the Tirah expedition is the record of an army which most manfully performed the arduous task apportioned to it; and conspicuous among all his comrades in that expedition, in courage and moral grandeur as well as in inches, *primus inter pares,* stands forth Lieutenant-Colonel John Haughton of the 36th Sikhs, a soldier *sans peur et sans reproche.* Were

I to quote here all that earlier writers have said in his honour and praise, I should fill many pages. I need not do so. Those whose love and regard for him are deep and lasting will have read and treasured all that has been said and written. To the majority of Englishmen, to whom the fame of their fellow-countrymen is dear, it will suffice to know the name of John Haughton as that of the man who won the right of being handed down to posterity as the hero of Tirah; and that without prejudice to hundreds of others whose deeds of bravery, whether recorded in public, treasured in private, or buried in seeming oblivion, are bearing their good fruit. No gallant deed is lost. If no other human eye sees it, the doer himself is the better man for it.

I think that I am entitled—I may say bound—to repeat here the brief encomia which the two chiefs under whom Lieut.-Colonel Haughton served during the Tirah expedition, the two last Commanders-in-Chief in India, have left on record regarding him in their respective despatches. General Sir W. S. A. Lockhart wrote, in reporting "The Shinkamar Affair:" "Among the killed, the country has to deplore the loss of Lieut.-Colonel Haughton, 36th Sikhs, an officer whose able and gallant leading of the fine regiment which he commanded had repeatedly come under my notice." General Sir George White in his despatch "deplored the loss to the army of so distinguished a soldier as Lieut.-Colonel Haughton, 36th Sikhs, whose career was so full of promise." It was further placed on record in the *London Gazette** that, had Lieut.-Colonel Haughton lived, he would have been recommended for some mark of Her Majesty's favour. As is well known, Her Majesty has had her own way of showing not only her favour, but also her sympathy.

In a little volume published in India by Major E. H. Rodwell, and not likely to have many, if any, readers in Great Britain, appears a brief but pregnant tribute to "the gallant Colonel Haughton, the Marshal Ney of the Tirah campaign." The simile is happy, and true of all but the last scene of life. A sage of old remarked that no man could be called fortunate until he was dead. Ney lived, even through the dangers of Waterloo, when he had five horses shot under him and his clothes riddled with bullets. It were better had fate willed that he should fall at the head of the Old Guard on that 18th of June. Haughton had the good fortune to die very nobly in action. His end was indeed *εὐθαναςία*, for death was instantaneous, and he died honoured and mourned by all. Contrast with this the obscure and ignoble death of General Skobeleff, brilliant and brave, but devoid of principle.

* Publishing the Tirah Despatch and Honours, under the date May 20, 1898.

CHAPTER I.

THE HAUGHTON AND PRESGRAVE FAMILIES.

"A people which takes no pride in the noble achievements of remote ancestors, will never achieve anything worthy to be remembered with pride by remote descendants."—MACAULAY.

WHEN a man wins for himself distinction in this world, there underlies the record of his lineage a higher interest and deeper import than those which the mere bare skeleton of a family tree can satisfy. A mere framework of names tells little or nothing. We desire to know what manner of men and women those ancestors were who wove the mental and moral fibre which, in the hour of stress, withstood the strain, and nerved the man for action.

I have before me many letters from John Haughton's best friends, and also the evidence of his own words and deeds; and from these I gather that the moral qualities which distinguished him were—high sense of duty, conscientious industry and application, strong religious feeling, staunchness, cool courage, resource in danger, modesty, courtesy, gentleness, geniality, and readiness to sacrifice himself, be it in some trifling incident of daily life, or in the moment when self-sacrifice meant death. It is almost needless to say, however, that a man so staunch and steady as he in the hour of danger, was one whose character also had its stern side. Haughton's most intimate friend during his career as a soldier was his old brother officer in the 10th Bengal Infantry, Colonel C. H. Palmer. Let me quote his own words, written to me a few months ago—

"He (Haughton) was kindly and courteous to every one, but he would stand no nonsense, and could answer very curtly and brusquely to any one who attempted to take any liberty with him. He had naturally a short and quick temper, but was so kind and tender-hearted that he would forgive and look over any fault or offence *against himself*, but he would do his duty in a matter of duty, however painful to himself."

In these words we have an outline of the soft and stern sides of his disposition, and a sketch also of his moral character. Intellectually he was a man of more than average capacity. He was not a genius in the ordinary acceptation of the term, but he had the inspiration of genius in the hour of danger. Physically he was, with his six feet six inches of stature, a man of mark anywhere. There is a little anecdote in one of Colonel Palmer's letters which gives a vivid picture of Haughton's height. "He joined the 10th Bengal Infantry at Jalpaiguri in 1887. I well remember his joining. He turned up unexpectedly one morning when we were waiting for the 'Fall in' to sound. He was in white uniform, and we noticed his very tall figure a long way off. Some one jocularly remarked, 'Why, here's Kinchin-junga got loose.'" (Kinchinjunga's snow-clad summit, 28,000 feet high, could be occasionally seen from Jalpaiguri.) John Haughton was the tallest of a tall family. His younger brother Henry stood six feet three inches. His grandfather and father were each over six feet in height. From them, and especially from the latter, he inherited not only his commanding stature, but also those mental and moral qualities which made him the man and soldier he was. The same sterling attributes evinced themselves in his elder brother Richard, who fought out his gallant fight amid the climatic dangers and difficulties of the Western Dooars; and in the younger one, Henry, who at the early age of twenty-five succumbed to cholera. That disease would seem to have had a certain fatality for the family—in that the grand-uncle, Sir Graves Chamney Haughton, died of it in 1849, while Richard Haughton's recovery from it in 1889 was due mainly to his having lived for years in its midst, so that when it did grip him he knew well how to wrestle with it. His mother's brother, Captain D. K. Presgrave, commanding the 8th Bengal Infantry, died of it at Peshawar in October, 1862.

Lieut.-Colonel Haughton was descended, both on his father's and mother's sides, of an ancient and good lineage. The Irish branch of the Haughton family traces its descent to the De Hoghtons of

Hoghton Tower, who are reputed to have been settled in Lancashire since the Conquest. In old documents the name of the family is spelt indifferently Haughton, Houghton, Howghton, Hauton, Horton, and even Aulton, also De Haughton. A branch of the family was settled at Stamford in Rutlandshire in the sixteenth century.*

In the reign of Charles I. the representative of this branch was taken to Ireland and settled there. A letter written to General J. C. Haughton by his father contains the following statement:—

"According to family tradition, the first of the name (*i.e.* of the Irish branch) was in childhood brought to Ireland by Captain Hoyle and his wife, who were relatives of the Haughtons of Haughton Tower in Lancashire, with the intention of bringing him back when the 'troubles,' as the wars of the Commonwealth were called, were over. I know not where Captain Hoyle settled, nor anything more connected with the intermediate members of the line till the time of my grandfather,† who held the lands of Cool-a-

* In the Rev. C. Nevinson's "History of Stamford," p. 87, is the following passage: "A town-hall was erected in 1558 by the then Alderman John Haughton. It stood across the north end of the bridge, over an arch which spanned the passage, but being found to be an obstacle to the increasing traffic, it was removed in 1776 for the improvement of the thoroughfare, and the present town-hall near St. Mary's Church was erected in its stead." The same Alderman John Haughton is referred to in an extant autograph letter by Lord Burghley, Lord Treasurer under Queen Elizabeth, in the following words: "We understand that one — houghton who is now ye alderman of this town, doth continue in the town, and is serious to do his endeavour," etc., etc. William Cecil, Lord Burghley, inherited from his father and mother large estates near Stamford, and as a boy was educated at a school in that town. Throughout his life he was a benefactor to it. From Alderman John Haughton of Stamford descended Colonel John Haughton of Tirah.

† Richard Haughton.

kirke in the parish of Newcastle, co. Wicklow, on the estate of Earl Fitzwilliam. He had a large family of sons and daughters. Of the former my father was the second."

This second son was the great-grandfather of Lieut.-Colonel John Haughton, and a physician in Dublin in the latter half of the last century. He married Jane, the daughter of Edward Archer, Esq., of Mount John, co. Wicklow, and by her left several sons. The eldest, Richard, the grandfather of the subject of this memoir, became Professor of Oriental Languages at Addiscombe.* One of his pupils there (General B. H. Morton, late B.S.C., still living, one who knew three generations of Haughtons—the professor at Addiscombe, the defender of Charikar, and the brave pioneer of the tea industry in the Western Dooars) writes of him as a man of fine presence and a good scholar, who knew how to keep his pupils at Addiscombe, unruly as they were prone to be, in thoroughly good order. He was a man of strong character. To his son's published narrative of the siege of Charikar is appended a most interesting letter written to him

* He married Miss Baker, of Bally David, in co. Tipperary, who by her mother was related to Sir John Colpoys, Admiral of the Fleet at the mutiny of the Nore. The sister of this Sir John Colpoys married Mr. Griffith, whose son, Admiral Sir Edward Griffith, took the name of Colpoys-Griffith on succeeding to his uncle's property. It was this Sir Edward Colpoys-Griffith who gave young John Colpoys Haughton, the hero of Charikar, his introduction to the navy. Sir John Colpoys was also treasurer and afterwards governor of Greenwich Hospital. When his name was notified to King George III. for the governorship, His Majesty is said to have made the following note on the paper: "This is an appointment of merit. A better man and a better admiral does not exist."

(the professor) in May, 1842, by Major Eldred Pottinger from his place of imprisonment among the Afghans near Kabul. We can imagine what a year of anxiety 1842 was to Professor Haughton, as to thousands of others in England. His son, after his gallant defence of and marvellous escape from Charikar, was finally left a prisoner, severely wounded, among the Afghans, and remained in their hands till September, 1842, when Sir George Pollock and Sir William Nott reoccupied Kabul.

The professor at Addiscombe had a still more distinguished brother, Sir Graves Chamney Haughton, who was for many years Professor of Oriental Languages at Haileybury. He was born at Dublin in 1788, and, after being educated in England, obtained in 1808 a military cadetship on the Bengal Establishment of the H.E.I.C.S. In the seven years (1808–1815) which followed his arrival in India, he devoted himself to the study of Oriental languages, and attained the standard of the degree of honour or high proficiency in Arabic, Persian, Sanscrit, Hindustani, and Bengali. In 1815 he returned to England, and from 1817 to 1828 held, first the Assistant-Professorship and afterwards the Professorship of Oriental Languages in the East India College at Haileybury. During this period he published many excellent Oriental class-books. In 1819 he was elected an honorary M.A. of Oxford, and in 1821 a Fellow of the Royal Society. He was an original member and an energetic promoter of the Royal Asiatic Society. During the latter years of his life he devoted himself to the study of metaphysics and philology, in which latter field he must have been one of the earliest English workers. In 1833 he was created a Knight of the Guelphic Order. He spent much of his later life in Paris, where he fell a victim to cholera at St. Cloud on August 28, 1849. He was a man whose studies, as his published works show, covered a very wide area of learning and thought, embracing philosophy, philology, science, medicine, and metaphysics.

On the mother's side Lieut.-Colonel Haughton was descended from the family of Presgrave, which can trace its descent back through the Presgraves of Bourne, Clerks of Penicuik, Rattrays of Craighall, and Stewarts, Lords of Kinfauns, to Joan Beaufort (granddaughter of John of Gaunt), who married (1) James I. of Scotland and (2) the Earl of Athole. His mother, Jessie Eleanor, was the eldest daughter of Colonel Duncan Presgrave and sister of Captain Duncan Kyd Presgrave, both officers of the Bengal Staff Corps, and both men who in their own particular line made their mark. Colonel Duncan Presgrave was one of those men such as might be found in the first half of the nineteenth century, who came to India and never thought of revisiting their native land. He spent forty years in India without taking leave, and when, in 1841, a paralytic stroke obliged him to seek a change of climate, it was only to reach the Cape of

THE FIRST SUSPENSION BRIDGE IN INDIA, BUILT OVER THE BEAS RIVER BY COLONEL DUNCAN PRESGRAVE.

(From an old photograph by Lieut.-Colonel John Haughton.)

Good Hope, and die there. He was a man of versatile abilities. Engineering talent ran strong in the Presgraves. After being for years mint-master at Saugor, he was selected by Government to fill the post of superintendent of the Cossipore Foundry, an appointment then usually given to an artillery officer.

The engineering feat for which Colonel Presgrave is noted, is the construction, in 1828–30, of a suspension bridge over the Beas, twelve miles from Saugor. This bridge is said to be the only suspension bridge in India made of Indian iron and constructed by Indian workmen. These workmen were taught by Colonel Presgrave himself. In March, 1893, Lieut.-Colonel John Haughton visited this bridge, and has left on record this description of it :—

"I was rather unexpectedly ordered to the artillery camp of exercise near Saugor. I took the opportunity to visit and photograph the iron suspension bridge over the Beas river, twelve miles from Saugor. Unfortunately, I had not a pencil with me to take down the inscriptions, of which one is to the following effect: 'Beas Suspension Bridge, designed and constructed by Major Presgrave, Assay-Master, Saugor Mint; commenced 1828, completed 1830.' The other is to the effect that the work was entirely carried out by local native workmen from iron ore found and smelted in the district. When one considers that our grandfather was not an engineer by profession, and had never seen a suspension bridge, and when one further considers how stupid native workmen are about any work they are unaccustomed to, one is struck with astonishment and admiration at this work. The bridge was never intended for heavy weights, and looks very fragile, but now, after so many years (without, I believe, any material repairs), was able to stand the strain of a whole battery of artillery crossing it. They, of course, crossed one gun at a time, but each gun with horses and men weighs, I believe, about six tons."

Captain Duncan Kyd Presgrave (born in 1829) inherited his father's engineering talent, and when a boy of sixteen was bound to the well-known civil engineer, Sir Robert Stephenson, for five years. However, a few months later, he was offered a direct commission in India by one of the Court of Directors of the H.E.I.C.S., and his guardians considered it best for him to accept it. He accordingly started for India, and in 1845 arrived in Calcutta. After declining, by Sir William Sleeman's advice, an appointment in the bodyguard of Sir Herbert Maddock, at that time Lieutenant-Governor of Bengal, he joined his regiment, the 59th N.I., which was then proceeding on active service, and with it served through the first Panjab campaign (1845–46). He subsequently, like many other officers of the Bengal army, passed into civil employ in the Panjab, and continued in it till the outbreak of the Mutiny in 1857. Like his father, he had a natural talent for engineering. Of that I can quote no better proof than a letter written to him when assistant-commissioner at Jullundur in March, 1855, by Mr. (afterwards Sir Donald and Lieutenant-Governor of the Panjab) McLeod:—

"MY DEAR PRESGRAVE,

"Allow me to convey to you my heartfelt congratulations on the very gratifying intelligence conveyed by your letter of the 26th, of the complete success of your girders to be, and of your having thus become the pioneer in the matter of girder bridges for the Panjab at all events, and I believe that in the whole of Hindoosthan no similar undertaking has hitherto been accomplished. I hope that this will be the beginning of a new era for the crossing of our wider spans, and I shall anxiously await the results of the official announcement. I have to thank you also for a copy of the pamphlet regarding your father's beautiful bridge over the Beas, of the construction of which I was myself in some sort a witness, as it was opened but partly when I joined at Saugor, and there remained much more still to be done to it, in which I used to take a great interest. In building the first iron girders in India you have followed worthily in the steps of the distinguished man who constructed the first and only suspension bridge made of Indian iron.

"(Signed) D. MCLEOD."

In 1857, when the Mutiny broke out, Captain Presgrave happened to be on sick leave at Simla. He at once gave up his leave, and instead of rejoining his civil appointment in the Panjab, came down to Delhi and volunteered for service with the 75th Regiment, now the 1st Battalion of the Gordon Highlanders. This regiment played a very prominent and distinguished part in the suppression of the Mutiny, and with it Captain Presgrave served throughout, as may be seen from the following extract from a letter written by Major F. S. (now Lord) Roberts to Captain Presgrave's widow (to whom and to whose children he has always been a kind and steadfast friend), dated Meerut, March 15, 1863:—

"Shortly after the Mutiny broke out in 1857, the late Captain Presgrave was, I believe, on sick leave at Simla. He gave up his leave and came down to Delhi, where he volunteered for H.M.'s 75th Regiment, with which he served throughout the campaign. The part taken by this distinguished regiment is too well known to need a fresh account from me. Suffice it to say, that Captain Presgrave was associated with it on all occasions: at the siege and assault of Delhi; actions of Boolundshahr, Allyghur, and Agra; advance on Lucknow, and occupation of Alumbagh, in which place H.M.'s 75th Regiment remained throughout the cold weather of 1857–58. Captain Presgrave was holding an appointment under the civil Government of the Panjab before the outbreak; this he preferred giving up to leaving the army while employed in the field. It was, of course, a great loss to him; for on the restoration of peace he was without an appointment, and remained so until his Excellency, General Sir Hugh Rose, became Commander-in-Chief. On hearing of the peculiar circumstances of the case, and being anxious to reward so gallant an officer, his Excellency gave the command of the 8th Native Infantry to Captain Presgrave, which command that officer held until his death by cholera, at Peshawur, in October, 1862."

To this testimony let me add those of Sir Hugh Rose and Sir Sydney Cotton, two officers who, the one actively in Central India, the other in the less conspicuous but scarce less onerous post of the Peshawar command, played a foremost part in suppressing the Mutiny. It is to Sydney Cotton, coupled with Herbert Edwardes and John Nicholson, that we largely owe the maintenance of order in the Panjab in 1857. Without such men, and others like them to support him, John Lawrence could never have done what he did. The light of Sydney Cotton is one that has lain under a bushel, but it was a noble and strong light for all that. The retention of Peshawar and the disarmament of the native troops there were the work of Herbert Edwardes and Sydney Cotton. Their firmness kept the Afghans quiet. Had this not been so, John Nicholson could not have led to Delhi that Brigade which first turned the scale there in favour of the British arms.

"Headquarters, Simla, October 8, 1863.

"The Commander-in-Chief in India has much pleasure in bearing testimony to the services of the late Captain Presgrave while in command of the 8th Native Infantry. Captain Presgrave served in the Sutlej campaign in 1845 and 1846, and throughout the Mutiny. He, with a most laudable military spirit, volunteered his services with the army before Delhi, throwing up an appointment which he held in the Panjab. Throughout the Mutiny he served with H.M.'s 75th Regiment. In recognition of his good services, Sir Hugh Rose gave him the command of the 8th Native Infantry, which he held until his death on October 21, 1862; and his Excellency was much satisfied with the manner in which Captain Presgrave exercised the command which he confided to him.

"(Signed) H. ROSE,
"General Commander-in-Chief, India."

Sir Sydney Cotton's testimonial is couched in

terms of greater warmth. Captain Presgrave served for some time under his personal command at Peshawar.

"Timperley Hall, Cheshire, March 28, 1866.

"Major Presgrave was a most valuable and most efficient officer. He served under my command on the Peshawur frontier, and, as commander of a regiment, rendered very important services to the State, by bringing into a high state of discipline and efficiency a new corps, raised at the expiration of the Mutiny of the old Sepoy Army of Bengal in 1857, and at a time when the native troops, who had rebelled against the Government, had to be replaced by corps composed of men on whom reliance could be placed. It was only by men such as Major Presgrave that this new order of things (of such vital importance to the State) could be accomplished, and well indeed did Major Presgrave discharge his duties up to the moment of his death, which was very sudden and unexpected. He died of spasmodic cholera. I do not herein advert to Major Presgrave's services at the siege of Delhi and elsewhere during the Mutiny, as he was not then under my immediate command, but I do know that Major Presgrave was in every respect a very serious loss to the service, and no one felt that or understood it better than myself. I know also that Major Presgrave relinquished the civil service and all its pecuniary advantages at a moment when his services as a soldier were required.

"(Signed) SYDNEY COTTON,
"Major-General, Commanding Northern District,
"Late Commander of the Peshawur Division, Bengal."

The 59th Bengal Native Infantry, the corps to which Captain D. K. Presgrave was originally appointed, and with which he served through the

Sutlej campaign, became after the Mutiny the 8th Native Infantry. Captain Presgrave's appointment to its command was in all respects appropriate, and, as we have evidence above, well deserved.

I have been able to give, from papers placed at my disposal by members of the Haughton and Presgrave families, this sketch, imperfect as it is, of the men who were the nearest relatives and immediate "forbears" of Lieut.-Colonel John Haughton. To his father, in whom I see more than in any other man the likeness, moral and physical, of the son, a separate chapter must deservedly be given. It is almost a recognized law of nature that the characteristics of the mother are reproduced in the son. We have not in this case the data on which to found any conclusions. Colonel Haughton's mother died on May 9, 1873, on her way home from India, at Castellamare, near Naples. She was necessarily, being with her husband in India, much separated from her children, who were brought up at home; but knowing as we do what manner of men her father, brother, and husband were, and what her three sons became, we may reasonably assume that she was a woman of some mark and character. When Lieutenant J. C. Haughton went home on leave after the first Afghan War, he met Miss Jessie Eleanor Presgrave at Brussels; and when, in 1845, she came out to Calcutta with her brother (Captain D. K. Presgrave), he proposed for and was accepted by her. The marriage took place at Calcutta on June 16, 1845. She became the mother of four children: Richard, born May 7, 1848, at Chyebassa, near Chhota Nagpur; Susan,* born June 10, 1850, at the Cape of Good Hope; John, born August 22, 1852, at Chhota Nagpur; Henry Lawrence, born October 1, 1857, at Tavoy. The name given to the last is, obviously, in memory of the noble soldier who fell in the defence of Lucknow a few months before; a man whom Lieutenant J. C. Haughton must have met and known during the first Afghan War, and whom he, like every other Indian soldier, had in his time revered as one of the finest characters the army has produced. His namesake, short as his life was, showed himself worthy of the name given him. John was in many respects his father's replica; and Richard, the eldest, was, as we will show later on, cast in a very similar mould.

* Married the Rev. Charles Halford Hawkins, M.A., for more than thirty years a master at Winchester School, and as such most highly esteemed.

CHAPTER II.

GENERAL JOHN COLPOYS HAUGHTON.*

"His signal deeds and prowess high
Demand no pompous eulogy—
Ye saw his deeds."

LONGFELLOW.

THE father of John Haughton was born at Dublin on November 25, 1817. He was an only son, though he had four sisters. Such brief scholastic education as he received was obtained at Shrewsbury School, under the then celebrated Dr. Samuel Butler (afterwards Bishop of Lichfield). He, however, left Shrewsbury, at the age of eleven, to be entered as a first-class volunteer on the books of H.M.S. *Magnificent*, the receiving ship at Jamaica. Admiral Sir Edward Colpoys-Griffith, at that time commanding the West Indian, North American, and

* Authorities consulted:—"War Services of all the Officers of Her Majesty's Bengal Army," compiled by Captain J. C. Anderson, 1863; Dictionary of National Biography, *sub voce;* Notices in the Overland and Homeward Mails and Indian Statesman of 1887; Kaye's "War in Afghanistan;" Lady Sale's Journal; "The Kabul Insurrection of 1841–42," by Sir Vincent Eyre; Stocqueler's "Memorials of Afghanistan;" "Memoir of Major Eldred Pottinger," by Kaye, in *Good Words* for 1866; John Colpoys Haughton's "Charikar," 1st edit. 1867, 2nd edit. 1879; "An Episode of the Afghan War," by Lieut. C. R. Low, in *Every Boy's Magazine*, September, 1877; "Memoir of Captain Augustus Abbott," published by Lieut. C. R. Low; Sir Henry Durand's "Afghan War;" Blue Book on Afghanistan, 1843, and private documents.

Newfoundland Station, was a relative of the Haughton family, and under his auspices young Haughton made his entry into the navy in 1829. He served as a midshipman in the navy (in H.M.'s Ships *Fly* and *Belvidera*) from 1829 to 1836, and in 1831–32 took part in the suppression of the negro rebellion in Jamaica. He was invalided from the navy in 1836. Through the influence of his father and uncle with the Court of Directors of the H.E.I.C., he obtained, in February, 1837, a Bengal cadetship, and on December 9 of the same year, being then just twenty years of age, joined as an ensign the 31st Bengal Native Infantry.*

The policy which led to the first Afghan War was then being matured. In the summer of 1838 orders were issued for the concentration of the Army of the Indus at Firozpur. The 31st Bengal Native Infantry formed part of Major-General Nott's Brigade in that army. Ensign Haughton's experience of active service thus began early in his career. He accompanied his regiment in its march from Firozpur to Sukkur, and shared in the hardships and trials of the advance across the Kachchi desert and up the Bolan Pass to Quetta in the winter of 1838–39. Our troops were harried all the way by Baluch and Brahui marauders, and sorely tried by the intense cold and the dearth of supplies. The Bengal Division, under Sir Willoughby Cotton, which had left Firozpur on December 18, 1838, equipped with a luxury that in these days excites

* Now the 2nd (Queen's Own) Rajputs.

wonder,* reached Quetta on March 26, 1839, almost in a state of starvation. Mr. Stocqueler tells how at Firozpur an officer declined his offer of a few boxes of cheroots, with the remark, "Oh, thanks! our mess has two camel-loads of the best Manillas;" whereas, on arrival at Quetta, there was "not a drop of beer with the army," and both men and animals were on half or even quarter rations.

It is no easy matter, with the most careful study of the numerous writers on the first Afghan War, to trace the doings of any particular corps. The 31st Bengal Native Infantry evidently left Quetta with Sir John Keane's column in April, 1839, and was probably detached to garrison some point on the communications between Quetta and Ghazni; for it was not present at the siege of Ghazni. When Major-General Willshire was directed to attack Kelat and depose its chief, Mehrab Khan, the 31st Bengal Native Infantry formed part of the force under his command. It marched with him from Quetta on November 3, 1839, and on the 13th of the same month co-operated with the 2nd and 17th Foot in storming Kelat. The storming column of the three regiments, having driven the Baluchis from the hills covering the city, followed the retreating enemy so closely and rapidly that they succeeded in entering the gate of the fortified town before it could be closed. The town being occupied, our troops then assailed the citadel, and forced an

* *Vide* Stocqueler's "Memorials of Afghanistan" and Sir Charles Napier's "Life."

entrance to it. A hand-to-hand fight then ensued, in which Mehrab Khan and many Baluch and Brahui chiefs were slain. A little later the 31st Bengal Native Infantry was attacked in camp by Mehrab Khan's defeated troops, who continued to infest the country between Quetta and Dadur until the close of the campaign. The attack was successfully repulsed. It would appear that Ensign Haughton was with the 31st Bengal Native Infantry during these operations, though he is stated to have been appointed on March 5, 1839, to be the adjutant of a provisional battalion of Shah Shuja's * contingent. It was in this capacity, doubtless, that he took part in the action of "Tazee" on May 10, 1840. The Ghilzais having again raised the standard of rebellion (the first outbreak had been crushed by Captain Outram in 1839), and assembled in force at Tazee, Captain Anderson, of the Bengal Horse Artillery, with four guns, 800 infantry, and 360 Irregular Horse, attacked and defeated them there, inflicting considerable loss. General Nott then arrived from Kandahar with reinforcements, and put an end to the insurrection. Soon after this, Ensign Haughton must have proceeded to Kabul and joined Shah Shuja's 4th or Gurkha Regiment of Infantry. This corps, raised by Major

* "Shuja'-ud-daulah" was the court title or official designation of the Afghan prince of the Saddozai family, whose cause the Government of India found it convenient to espouse, as a pretext for attacking the Amir Dost Mohammed Khan. He was a refugee in 1838 at Ludhiana. Some of his descendants are, or were very recently, serving in the ranks of our Native Army in India.

McSherry, of the 30th Bengal Native Infantry, in the summer of 1838, and composed originally of Gurkhas and hill-men from Kumaon, had accompanied Sir John Keane to Ghazni, taking part in the fighting both there and on the way there. On September 12, 1839, this regiment formed part of a small force despatched from Kabul to hold Bamian. It was then commanded by Captain Hay, with Lieutenant William Broadfoot as second in command, and Lieutenant Golding as adjutant. Detachments of it were subsequently pushed forward to Syghan and Bajgah, amid the difficult passes of the Hindu Kush, and there they held their own, fighting continually with Dost Mohammed's Uzbeg troops and the local clans until August, 1840. On the news that Dost Mohammed was advancing with a large force, these detachments fell back on the main body at Bamian. Meanwhile Colonel Dennie left Kabul with reinforcements, and, arriving at Bamian early in September, assumed command. On September 17, hearing that the enemy's advanced troops were within striking distance, Colonel Dennie moved out with nine hundred men, and, to his surprise, found himself face-to-face with Dost Mohammed's entire force.* Without hesitation he

* Military officers in Afghanistan were even more dependent on the political authorities for information in the first than in the second Afghan War. Colonel Dennie's situation at Bamian in September, 1840, is analogous to that of General Burrows at Maiwand in July, 1880. In both cases political information seriously under-estimated the enemy's forces. Colonel Dennie, confronted unexpectedly with greatly superior numbers, by the promptitude of his attack won victory. General Burrows courted and suffered defeat by remaining on the defensive in a singularly ill-chosen position.

led his troops to the attack, and won a decisive victory, to which the Gurkhas contributed by their courage and *élan.* Dost Mohammed fell back on Khulm, and Colonel Dennie, in accordance with his orders, withdrew the Bamian force, including the Gurkhas, to Kabul. Captain Hay, whose health had broken down, was now succeeded in the command by Captain Codrington. Such, briefly, was the career of Shah Shuja's Gurkha regiment, up to the time when Ensign (or Lieutenant, as he is now termed by every writer, though he was not gazetted Lieutenant till July 16, 1840) Haughton joined it. After passing the winter of 1840–41 at Kabul, the regiment was ordered to occupy Charikar, in the Kohistan, with a view to dominating that disaffected district, in which insurrection had been put down with a strong hand the previous autumn by a brigade under Sir Robert Sale. The Ex-Amir Dost Mohammed Khan had, it is true, most unexpectedly surrendered himself to Sir William Macnaghten in November, 1840, and had been deported to India; but his son, Mohammed Akbar Khan, a dangerous enemy, was at large in Badakhshan, and the Kohistanis were known to be, to a man, his partisans.

Charikar lies forty miles due north of Kabul, as the crow flies, and is a most important strategical point, commanding the junction of several passes over the Hindu Kush with the roads leading to Bamian, Kabul, and through Nijrao to Jalalabad. The place had been held all the winter by the

Kohistan Rangers, under Lieutenant Maule of the Bengal Artillery. Here, as elsewhere, the authorities had tried the impossible experiment of enlisting Afghan Irregulars in the so-called service of our puppet Shah Shuja—irregulars who invariably deserted or even turned upon us on the first opportunity. To raise a corps of Kohistanis to keep their own fellow-rebels in order was certainly a remarkable thing to attempt. A sense of the untrustworthiness of the Kohistan Rangers, as well as apprehension of what Mohammed Akbar Khan might do, no doubt induced Macnaghten and Elphinstone to send the Gurkhas to Charikar and move the Rangers back to Kardarrah, about half-way betwen Charikar and Kabul. The officers then with the Gurkhas were—Captain Codrington (commandant), Lieutenant Haughton (adjutant), Ensign Salisbury (quartermaster), and Ensign Rose (subaltern).* There were also two British non-commissioned officers, Sergeant-Major Byrne and Quartermaster-Sergeant Hanrahan. On its arrival at Charikar the Gurkha regiment found neither barracks nor defences. Officers and men all remained under canvas for some months, while the quasi-fortified barracks which had been commenced by Lieutenant Maule and his Kohistanis were being completed by the Gurkhas. As a matter of

* Lieutenant W. Broadfoot, the second in command, was with Sir Alex. Burnes in Kabul, and was there murdered with him on November 2, 1841, the day before Rattray was shot down at Charikar. Thus, as will be seen later on, the only British officer of this regiment who lived to return to India was Lieutenant Haughton.

fact, they never were completed. The insurrection which broke out in and around Kabul at the beginning of November, 1841, found Captain Codrington and his regiment anything but prepared for a defence. A plot of ground about a hundred yards square had been enclosed by mud walls "from seven to twenty feet high," on the inside of which flat-roofed rooms for the men had been built. The officers' quarters were on the west side. Each corner of the enclosure was bastioned after the manner of the native forts. There was no water-supply in the fort. That from the canal or from the Khwāja-seh-yāran stream could be cut off at once by a besieging enemy. The eastern entrance had no gate, and the quarters had no doors. The interior of the barrack square was commanded from the trees that bordered the canal, a hundred yards distant, and by the high towers of Khwaja Mir Khan's fort, distant four hundred yards. Although "Brown Bess" in those days had only an effective range of about two hundred yards, the Afghan jezail was effective at six hundred yards, according to Sir Sydney Cotton, or even up to eight hundred, according to Captain Augustus Abbott. Kaye and Eyre both describe the Afghans as laughing at our musket-fire, and in 1842 the Adjutant-general of the Bengal army proposed to arm our troops with jezails instead of muskets.* It will thus be seen that Khwaja Mir Khan's fort, in

* *Vide* "Sixty Years of Frontier Warfare," in the *Journal of the Royal U.S. Institution* for March, 1900, pp. 238, 239.

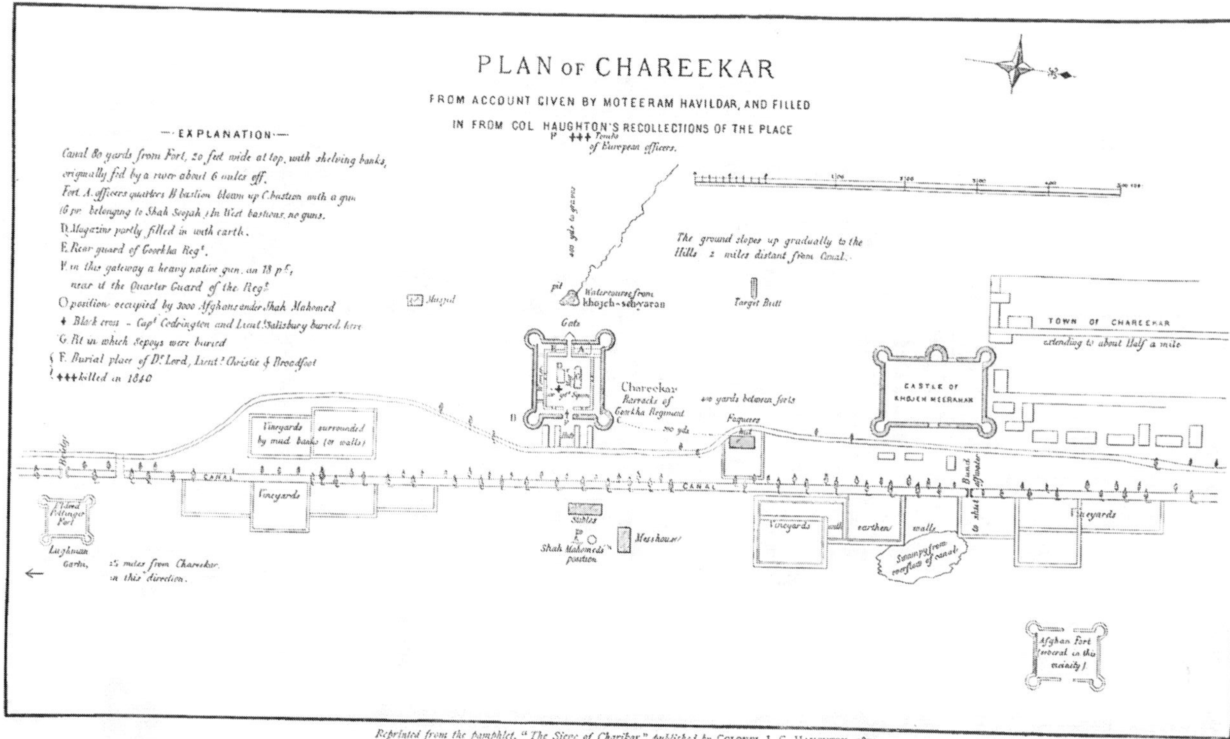

Reprinted from the pamphlet, "The Siege of Charikar," published by COLONEL J. C. HAUGHTON, 1879.

the hands of an enemy, would seriously menace the security of the Gurkha barracks. The masjid, target-butt, banks of the canal and trees bordering it, walled vineyards and gardens, the mess-house, stables and huts for married sepoys, and the fakir's hut, all afforded cover to assailants (*vide* plan attached).

About two and a half miles to the south (*i.e.* on the Kabul side) of Charikar lay a fortified native residence, called Lughmani or Lughman Ghari. In this dwelt the political agent, Major Eldred Pottinger, the gallant defender of Herat in 1837 against the Persians. With him was his assistant, Lieutenant Rattray, Dr. Grant, a company of Gurkhas, and a number of Afghan levy-men.

The rising of the Kohistanis commenced at Lughmani. Warning had not been wanting. Indeed, both Eldred Pottinger in the Kohistan and Henry Rawlinson at Kandahar had long been warning the envoy, Sir William Macnaghten, that there was no loyalty towards Shah Shuja among the Afghans. But the envoy pooh-poohed them as alarmists. He little foresaw that he was paving the way for his own fate and that of the whole army of occupation at Kabul.

Whether Major Eldred Pottinger was fully aware of the danger that was impending, cannot now be ascertained. Probably he was not. It seems certain that on the 2nd, if not on the 1st of November, Mir Masjidi, the most turbulent of the Kohistani chiefs, was already on the move from

Nijrao, across the plain of Barikat, with thousands of followers, and by the morning of November 3, if not earlier, had taken up a position at Aksarai, barring the road to Kabul. Had Pottinger been cognizant of this move—as, according to Kaye and Eyre, he was—would he, on November 3, have admitted, as he did, a number of Kohistani maliks or head-men to his fort, and others of minor standing into his garden? And would he have allowed his assistant, Lieutenant Rattray, to go outside the fort with some of these maliks? Rattray, once outside, was treacherously shot down. At the sound of firing, the chiefs who were with Major Pottinger in the garden rose and fled, while he himself escaped by the postern gate into the fort. His Gurkha guard at once turned out, and manning the walls, checked the attack with which the fort was threatened, and cleared the open ground of the Kohistanis, who then, taking cover in ditches and behind walls, continued to harry the defenders of the fort, or rather of the four small forts or enclosures, occupied by the political agent with his escort and following. Captain Codrington had gone, as it chanced, that morning from Charikar to Lughmani to see Major Pottinger, and was with him when Rattray was shot down. Lieutenant Haughton at Charikar, hearing the sound of firing (at about 2 p.m.), started off at once with 120 rifles, and finding the Pathans swarming among the walled gardens round Pottinger's fort, charged and drove them out. Codrington at the same time sallied forth and effected a junction with Haughton. It was by this time beginning to get dark; so, having strengthened the garrison of Lughmani to 120 men, and having arranged to send Major Pottinger some provisions and ammunition at dawn on the following day, Codrington returned with Haughton and his men to Charikar.

It was probably on November 3 that the Kohistan Rangers rose at Kardarrah, murdered their commandant (Lieutenant Maule), adjutant (Lieutenant Wheeler), sergeant-major, and quarter-master-sergeant, and then marched off to join Mir Masjidi and swell the thousands already thronging round Charikar. Lieutenant Rattray's Afghan levies at Lughmani, who throughout the year 1840 at Bamian, and subsequently at Charikar, had remained faithful, deserted and joined the rebels, as soon as their quondam chief was shot down.

Kaye, Eyre, Pottinger, Stocqueler, Haughton, and Low have all told the tale of the defence of Charikar. From me only a brief summary is needed. The siege lasted from the 4th to the 13th of November. Had the garrison been well posted, and supplied with water, food, and ammunition, its fate would have only been postponed. The help that was hoped for from Kabul was hoped for in vain; for Kabul was in only less dire straits than Charikar. Had Sir William Macnaghten and General Elphinstone been made of the same stuff as Eldred Pottinger and John Colpoys Haughton,

Kabul and perhaps Charikar also might have been saved. General Elphinstone was a broken-down invalid, while Macnaghten was one of those clever emanations of an Indian Secretariat, whom Viceroys and Members of Council sometimes delight to honour. He was a man without ballast, making his wish the father to his thought, turning a deaf ear to the earnest warnings of his subordinates, at one moment seeing all things *couleur de rose*, at another querulously charging his political and military assistants alike with incapacity. Unfortunately, he was able to work the ruin of more than one good staunch soldier. In 1841 the Political Service in India still exercised that control over troops in the field which the Duke of Wellington, writing to Lord Ellenborough in April, 1843, so strongly condemned, and which now, happily, is no longer allowed, although there is undue interference still. The political officer's duties should now be consigned to the Intelligence and Commissariat Departments. The political officer on active service is no longer needed, if indeed he was *ever* needed. The combined incapacity and inaction of Macnaghten and Elphinstone placed Major Eldred Pottinger and Shah Shuja's Gurkhas in an indefensible position, and gave them, as a support, a corps (the Kohistan Rangers) which could not be trusted, and which, when the outbreak in and around Kabul did take place, by revolting deprived the garrison of Charikar of its sole chance of escape. It remains now only to tell how for ten days they struggled against the thousands (twenty to twenty-five thousand is the variously estimated number) who hemmed them in, against the tortures of thirst, and against the exhaustion of hunger; for though they had food, it could not be cooked or eaten without water.

On November 4, before dawn, Haughton, accompanied by Ensign Salisbury and Quartermaster-Sergeant Hanrahan, one 6-pounder gun, and two hundred Gurkhas, started for Lughmani. Several ponies, loaded with provisions and ammunition, went with him. As Lughmani was approached, seven or eight hundred Afghans were seen on the right. Ensign Salisbury was detached to hold them in check, while Haughton carried out his duty of handing over the supplies and ammunition to Major Pottinger. The Afghans, however, now commenced to swarm in from all sides, and Haughton had to send Quartermaster-Sergeant Hanrahan to extricate Salisbury. Haughton meantime was halted five hundred yards from Lughmani, waiting in vain for the party which, as arranged, was to come out and take over the supplies and ammunition. Finally, he was obliged, to prevent his retreat being cut off, to retire on Charikar. The country was alive with the enemy. When Salisbury did return, hard pressed by the Afghans, Quartermaster-Sergeant Hanrahan was severely wounded, and many men had fallen. The 6-pounder gun was their salvation, for the enemy feared to close with that. This gun, Haughton, aided by a few men, most gallantly worked throughout the retreat of three miles. Salisbury, however, was mortally wounded, and many Gurkhas fell. None who fell could be saved.

After Haughton's return, measures were taken by Captain Codrington and him to prepare to stand a siege. All provisions were brought inside the square. A Subedar and fifty rifles were posted in the tower of Khwaja Mir Khan's fort, which commanded the barracks at a range of four hundred yards. On examining the provisions and stores of ammunition, they found that they had food for seven days, two hundred rounds per musket, and about sixty rounds per gun. When these were, later on, exhausted, old lead, nails, copper money, links of chain and blank cartridges were used in lieu of grape and canister for the guns.

By the afternoon the Gurkha barracks were hemmed in on all sides. Desultory fighting went on till dark. The Afghans cut off the water-supply. From that time the garrison was dependent on a few pools left in the bed of the canal and in a small pit near the barracks, from which earth had been dug to make bricks.

About 9 p.m. Haughton started with a single orderly to reconnoitre towards Lughmani, in the hopes of being able to communicate with Pottinger. Before he had gone far, sounds indicated that a party of some sort, friend or foe, was approaching. To his joy, he found it was Major Pottinger and all his following. Convinced that his position at

Lughmani was untenable, and relief improbable, Pottinger had decided to make an effort to gain Charikar by stealth, abandoning almost all the baggage. Fortune favoured him. The Afghans had not invested Charikar so closely as they did a day or two later. Thus the whole British force was able to unite and live or die together. It was mostly to die. The joy of escape was, however, marred by finding that some of Pottinger's Gurkha escort were missing. Two nights later they turned up, having held their own without food and water against the Afghans, who feared to attack men accessible only by a ladder and through a trap-door, and who probably abstained from burning them out in the firm assurance that they must very soon be starved out.

November 5 was one stern struggle for existence from morning to night. The Afghans, at least twenty thousand in number, swarmed to the attack from all sides. "Their very numbers," says Haughton in his account, "gave us nerve." The garrison still hoped for relief from Kabul. Major Pottinger on his arrival had at once volunteered for service, and, being an artillery officer, was instructed to take charge of the guns. Captain Codrington continued to exercise the command. The rules of the service, even in those days, did not allow a political officer to avail himself of his superior rank to supersede a military officer; though Major Pottinger had no such thought. The same spirit animated him that made Viscount Hardinge serve as a volunteer under Gough in the Panjab, and Outram under Havelock in the Mutiny.

The main object of the garrison was to keep their hold on the canal for the sake of the pools of water in it. Therefore the gardens and vineyards along the canal banks were occupied and tenaciously held. Here Haughton remained all day, ever on the move from one point to another. For he found that when he or some other British officer or non-commissioned officer was not there, the Gurkhas showed a tendency to yield before the thousands that threatened them. Codrington was in chief command, Pottinger worked the guns from the barracks, Salisbury was dying, and Hanrahan incapacitated by his wound. Haughton and Rose and Sergeant-Major Byrne were the only three Englishmen available to keep the Gurkha picquets staunch. So Haughton never left his outposts. In the forenoon came the intelligence that Pottinger was severely wounded in the thigh. At noon came the still graver news that Codrington had fallen. It was not, however, till dusk that Haughton felt justified in leaving his post and going to see Codrington. He found him shot through the chest and dying. The parting scene between them was a most affecting one, but duty made it imperative for Haughton to return to his outposts. With them he stayed all night. He has recorded that throughout the siege, and for a week or two after it, sleep entirely left him. "My usual post at night, when not moving about, was in a chair near the east gate" (the 18-pounder gun was there), "where I soothed my nerves with a cheroot."

At daybreak on the 6th, the Afghan attack recommenced with renewed vigour. The Gurkhas, under Haughton, Rose, and Byrne, fought all day, but in the evening were compelled to withdraw from the outposts in the gardens. Their numbers were much diminished, and the men worn out by fasting and fatigue; furthermore, the pools in the canal were now empty. During the day Sergeant-Major Byrne was mortally wounded, and Codrington breathed his last. Salisbury had passed from unconsciousness to death the previous afternoon. Secretly and silently, on the night of the 6th, Haughton, Grant, and Rose dug a grave and committed to it the remains of Codrington and Salisbury. The grave was smoothed down and straw burnt over it, as Haughton wished to keep the sad news as much as possible from his men. Haughton had had the narrowest escapes. One Pathan shot at him at two paces' distance and missed him. Again a bullet passed through his orderly's head and struck him so severely on the throat that he fell paralyzed. His men were dragging both away for dead, by the legs, when Haughton came to and objected to that mode of progression. They then lifted his head too. He soon recovered and resumed his duties. When night fell, he went to the doctor, who examined his neck. The thick silk Multani handkerchief he wore had saved him from anything more than an abrasion and momentary loss of power.

On the 7th the enemy formed a complete cordon round the barracks, keeping just out of musket-range. They took cover in the vineyards and canal-bed, in the stables and mess-house, behind the target-butt and in the fakir's hut and enclosure. Bullets began to drop in the interior of the barrack square; and it was presently ascertained that they came from Khwaja Mir Khan's fort, the garrison of which had surrendered. Bullets also came in freely through the east gate. The only available form of traverse was to use the walls of tents as screens. These were put up along the north wall and behind the men defending the south wall, and just inside the east gate. They could not stop bullets, but they stopped the firing of the enemy, who did not care to fire aimlessly.

On the 8th the Afghans made overtures, under the pretext of arranging terms of surrender, and several of them were admitted to see Major Pottinger. It was felt, however, that they were rather spies than envoys, and treachery was feared. Their presence, too, had no good effect on the Gurkhas. During the day the garrison buried the dead, forty-four in all. All who fell outside the walls had to lie unburied, as well as the horses and cattle. The stench from them became abominable. The siege had now changed from an active attack into a passive beleaguerment. The enemy formed a complete cordon round the barracks, keeping well under cover, and harrying the defenders with their fire as opportunity offered. All night drums were beat to worry and wear out the garrison, by keeping it continually on the alert. This drum-beating was done by the Afghan non-combatants, while the warriors took their rest. On the 9th Haughton was struck on the elbow by a spent ball. A painful bruise was the only result. On the night of the 9th loud singing commenced opposite the south-east corner, and soon after midnight an explosion took place. The enemy simultaneously opened fire from all sides, but did not attempt an assault. Had they done so, they would probably have carried the place in the confusion. Haughton, with his reserve, was at the breach in a moment or two, and barricaded it. It transpired that a Pathan had crept up to the bastion, dug a hole,* filled it with powder, tamped and exploded it. The singing was to drown the noise of digging. Precautions were now taken to prevent this recurring.

On the 11th the last drop of water was doled out. Hindus as these Gurkhas were, and sensitive on all points of caste, they yet begged that Haughton himself should divide fairly and distribute the little water left. Such was the faith of the Indian in British impartiality. The sheep belonging to the officers' mess were now given to the Gurkhas; but they said they could not eat the meat, as it only made them more thirsty. Many sucked the raw flesh to assuage their thirst. Signs of disaffection among the Mohammedan gunners began to show

* It was in this way that the now famous Saragarhi Post was taken in September, 1897.

themselves. One had deserted, and the others had all asked for their pay, though they could have no possible use for it. On the nights of the 11th and 12th, sorties were made in order to obtain water. The result was a severe conflict with the Pathan picquets, who were surprised and suffered heavily; but no water was brought in. On the 13th it became perfectly evident that, there being no water, the garrison could not hold out longer. A council was held in Major Pottinger's room. It was decided that the only plan that promised any chance of success was to endeavour to reach Kabul, avoiding the main road. The start was fixed for midnight.

Of the original garrison of 740 men ("of whom half were recruits," says Haughton) fully 100 had now been killed and 50 taken prisoners, while some 200 wounded thronged eight of the barrack-rooms. Thus less than 400 men, exhausted with fatigue and privation, remained. There were also about 100 women, 40 children, and 100 followers. Of the 56 Punjabi gunners 12 had been killed: Haughton had been warned that the remainder were not to be trusted, but he could not afford either to arrest them or turn them out of barracks. As events proved, he paid dearly for his dependence on them.

Towards the afternoon of the 13th he went up on to the north-east bastion to find out the reason for a sudden cessation in the firing. Ensign Rose went with him, and the subadar of artillery followed. A man was seen approaching the barracks. He turned out to be the artillery deserter. To quote Haughton's own account:—

"It was plain that the enemy had sent him, probably to offer terms; and as I was quite determined not to make any, being completely assured that none made with us would be kept, I felt it of importance to prevent his holding any communication with the men. At this time I was unarmed. I met the man as he came in, and seized him by the collar with my left hand as he attempted to pass me. Instantly he threw himself on the ground, I still holding him. This reduced me to a stooping posture, in which I received a tremendous blow on the neck, which I conjecture was followed by one or two more. I started, letting go my man and turning round, at the same time feeling a sharp pain in my right wrist. I saw the blood spouting in a long jet from it and the subadar glaring at me like a demon, holding a sword with both hands and in the act of striking at me again. All this was the work of an instant. I had the whole of the muscles on one side of the back of my neck severed, a severe cut into the right shoulder-joint, another in the right wrist nearly severing my hand, and a fourth in the left forearm splintering the bone. I retreated up a ladder to the roof of the barracks and shouted 'Treachery!' calling on the men to fire on the gunners who were escaping *en masse*. I, however, after having the limb with its spouting artery bound, found myself so faint from loss of blood that I could not stand. I was conducted between two men into the lower story of the building, in which was Pottinger, and was laid on a bed. The enemy made a most vigorous attack on all sides. Pottinger had himself carried to the gate where the doctor, with one or two men, vigorously worked the 18-pounder, and by dark the enemy had been completely repulsed. I heard afterwards that the artillerymen, seeing our affairs were desperate, thought it best to make terms for themselves. The arrangement was that they were to kill me, as a proof of their zeal, and go over to the enemy, who were to make a general attack in the confusion which would ensue, and take the place by escalade; it was expected no one would remain to work the guns. On this point, and in the anticipated success, calculations failed. It appears that from some sign the subadar understood all was settled. He, therefore, when I left his side, snatched a sword from the hands of Ensign Rose and followed me."

With the fall of Haughton discipline ceased to have any hold on the Gurkhas and followers. Men, women, and children loaded themselves with anything they could find. The money in the treasure-chest was divided. Dr. Grant spiked the guns; and when all was ready, the doctor amputated Haughton's right hand at the wrist-joint. The only liquid in the fort was some ether, and with that he was revived and stimulated. Set on a horse, with a man holding him on either side, he was led to the parade-ground, which had been selected as the place of rendezvous. Half the natives were not there. Time was too precious to allow of long waiting. The Gurkhas, moreover, were quite out of hand. The party marched off. At the first water many remained.* The numbers of the party

* It is known that 165 of these Gurkha soldiers rejoined, when Sir George Pollock reoccupied Kabul in September to October, 1842. Some few turned Mohammedans and settled in the Kohistan. It is evident that the Afghans spared many of these Gurkhas, and probably also of the women, children, and followers. Those spared would be forced to profess the Mohammedan faith. What became of the

gradually dwindled until only seven or eight were left. Major Pottinger, who knew that in speed and secrecy alone lay any chance of escape, determined to push on. When daylight broke the fugitives concealed themselves in a nullah. The party now consisted of Major Pottinger; Lieutenant Haughton; Mohan Bir, the major's munshi; Man Singh, Haughton's orderly,* and a native sutler. During the day parties of Afghans were seen searching the surrounding hills. One party came within 200 yards of their place of concealment, but turned back without seeing them. Their sole sustenance consisted of dried mulberries and water. The ether was used to sustain Haughton. At dark they started again, straight across the hills. They dare not follow the beaten tracks. Several times Haughton slipped off his horse, and in his helpless state suffered severely. He begged to be left to his fate, but Major Pottinger "nobly and generously" (to use Haughton's own words) "refused to do so." They passed a nomad encampment, unnoticed save

renegade Panjabis I have been unable to ascertain. Dr. Grant and Ensign Rose were both killed.

* To the end of his life General J. C. Haughton continued to take the deepest interest in this man. He was rather a rolling stone, but finally retired from the service of Government with a pension. In his letters to his son John at Benares, Banda, and Cawnpore, written between 1880 and 1887, the General asked him several times to ascertain from the Pension Paymaster where Man Singh was drawing his pension and how he was, but the son was unsuccessful in obtaining any news of him. He, however, reports to his father that Sir Herbert McPherson, and Colonel Hammond and Major Carr of the 5th Punjab Cavalry, had met near Kabul one or two Gurkhas who had survived the siege of Charikar. They told McPherson that two only of those who had remained behind in Afghanistan were then living.

by the barking of the dogs, and at last reached Deh-Afghan, a suburb of Kabul. There they were challenged, but pushing on escaped capture. They reached and entered the city of Kabul. Mohan Bir and the sutler sought refuge in the house of a Hindu whom they knew, but Man Singh declined to leave his master. The three—Pottinger, Haughton, and Man Singh—pushed on through the city into the lane leading to the British cantonment. There an Afghan picquet threatened, at the last moment, to frustrate all their hopes and efforts. But, as usual in the early hours of the morning, the picquet was asleep and the sentry drowsy. The fugitives in desperation urged on their weary steeds. Man Singh, who was on foot, managed to keep up with them. They were almost past the picquet when it turned out. A few shots were fired after them in the dark, and missed them. The pursuit died away. They were safe, though one other difficulty lay before them—the British outposts had also to be passed. The firing of the Afghan picquet had put them on the alert. No one of the three knew the countersign. This danger, however, was also overcome, and a few minutes later (as Sir Vincent Eyre wrote at the time inhis Journal) "they were received by their brethren in arms as men risen from the dead."*

* Major Eldred Pottinger remained a prisoner in the hands of Mohammed Akbar Khan when General Elphinstone's force evacuated Kabul in January, 1842. In September of that year he was rescued from his captivity, and returned to India with General Pollock. He was rewarded for his services with the Companionship of the Bath. His health obliged him to seek a change of climate.

The goal reached, they collapsed. On reaching the cantonment Haughton's wounds were, for the first time, properly dressed. His recovery was slow. On December 29, 1841, before General Elphinstone evacuated Kabul, "all the sick and wounded who were considered unable to bear the fatigues of the march were sent into the city (Kabul), and two medical officers, Doctors Berwick and Campbell, were appointed to take charge of them."* Lieutenant Haughton was one of these. There he remained till the end of August, when the advance of General Pollock obliged Mohammed Akbar Khan to retire from Kabul. Lady Sale, who was one of the prisoners, states in her "Journal" (p. 412) that most of the sick left at Kabul joined them at their place of captivity on August 20, 1841, and that Lieutenant Haughton and a few others were to follow as soon as transport could be obtained for their removal. From this it would seem that Lieutenant Haughton had not, even then, thoroughly recovered from his very severe wounds and from the terrible exposure and exertion which he had to go through, for forty hours after receiving his wound, in order to save his life. It was an abnormal test of strength of will and constitution. He, like the other prisoners, obtained his release on the approach of General Pollock's army. During Pollock's re-occupation of Kabul, he served with George Broadfoot's Sappers and

He died at Hong Kong on November 13, 1843, the first anniversary of his retreat from Charikar. There is a monument to his memory in the Cathedral at Bombay.

* Kaye, vol. ii. p. 182.

Miners (Gurkhas); 165 men of his old corps, who had escaped with their lives, came in and rejoined him, and with him returned to India in October, 1842. He was then at once sent home to recruit his health. While in England he was pressed to publish an account of the defence of Charikar, but declined. At Brussels he met the lady, Miss Jessie Eleanor Presgrave, whom he afterwards married at Calcutta in June, 1845. From that date, till his retirement from the service in 1873, she shared with him all the vicissitudes of an Indian career, but died within a few months of her return to Europe, at the age of forty-seven.

The Charikar episode was the stirring incident of General J. C. Haughton's life, but for thirty-two years after that he continued to serve the Government of India, and well he served it. In November, 1844, he was appointed second in command of the Bundelkhand Service Battalion, whence he was transferred, in 1846, to the Chhota Nagpur Commission. During the rebellion of Ghoomsoor, he served with the Ramghar Battalion, and was present in seven affairs with the enemy. From 1853 to 1862 he served in Burma and the Andaman Islands. In 1862 he was appointed Commissioner of Assam and Governor-General's Agent for the North-east Frontier. In 1862–63 he was engaged in the suppression of the rebellion in Jyntia, and at the end of 1864 he joined the Bhutan Field Force as chief civil and political officer, and remained with it till June, 1865, being present at the storming of

Dalimkot and the re-capture of Bala. For his services on this occasion he received the Companionship of the Order of the Star of India. In 1866 he was appointed the Commissioner of the Cooch-Behar Division, and held that appointment until his retirement in 1873. The following resolution was then issued by the Lieut.-Governor of Bengal:—

"Colonel J. C. Haughton, C.S.I., Commissioner of Cooch-Behar, having been forced by ill-health to leave the country, notwithstanding that the Secretary of State had agreed to an extension of his service in consequence of his merits, the Lieut.-Governor deems it right to express the thanks of the Government to this distinguished officer for his very long and meritorious services to the Government of Bengal. Colonel Haughton's services in Cabul, where severe wounds caused him the loss of an arm, were concluded before he joined the North-west Frontier Agency, under this Government, in the year 1844. Since that year he has, with intervals of employment under the Government of India at Port Blair and elsewhere, served in the wilder and more remote districts of Bengal—from Sumbalpor and Sungboom on the west, to Bootan on the north, and Upper Assam on the extreme east. In times of peace he has served the Government well, and has always shown the fullest consideration for the welfare and wants of all classes under his administration; he has always exerted his influence in behalf of the wilder races; he has contributed much to the pacific solution of questions regarding the treatment of the mountain tribes which inhabit the wilds on both sides of the Berampootra Valley, and his loss will be felt in future discussion on the Bootan frontier. In time of war and trouble on the British frontier towards Bhootan, in the Garrow Hills, in the Cossyah and Jyntia

Hills, he has personally done the very greatest services in advising and directing the operations, and by raising levies of hillmen for frontier police work or for the carriage of materials. His last piece of service has been to superintend, to a most successful termination, an expedition undertaken this cold season for the subjugation of the hitherto independent Garrows, who have long harassed our district; he has managed with success the large estate of the infant Maharajah of Cooch-Behar.

"The Lieut.-Governor would tender his thanks to Colonel Haughton for the good work he has done as a frontier officer, as a district officer, and as a commissioner during the last thirty years, and will bring them prominently to the notice of the Government of India and the Secretary of State."

This is but a lukewarm tribute to the merits of General Haughton compared with those which appeared in the Anglo-Indian press at the time of his death, which took place at Ramsgate on September 17, 1887. One writer speaks of his "great ability, firmness, and justice, combined with a high-minded gentleness which won the hearts of all, natives and Europeans." In person he is described as "over six feet in height, with a spare, wiry frame capable of great physical endurance, aquiline features and a kindly resolute face."

His friends felt that his services might have received some more substantial recognition than a mere C.S.I. For his services in the Afghan War he was not awarded even a medal. He was promised a brevet majority, but never received it. When, later on, shortly before the Mutiny, Captain Haughton

Lieut-General John Colpoys Haughton. C.S.I.

ventured to remind the authorities of this promise, he was met with those forms of red-tape obstruction which secretariats know so well how to use. I have before me a kind letter (private, not official) written to Captain J. C. Haughton by Colonel Chester from Simla on May 2, 1857, a few days before the mutiny at Meerut broke out, explaining to him that the Court of Directors would receive *memorials only*, not letters. At the end of this letter is the following note in Captain J. C. Haughton's handwriting:—

"This is from Colonel Chester, at that time Adjutant-General of the Indian Army. The memorial in triplicate was duly sent in and returned with intimation that it must be sent through the officer commanding the 54th Bengal Native Infantry, the regiment in the army list on which my name stood, and which I had never joined or seen in my life. The mutinies came on, and Colonel Chester was one of the first killed."

His own persevering representations, and those made by his father (the professor of Oriental languages at Addiscombe) on his behalf, failed to produce any effect. To a man in civil employ a brevet is of no practical use; but the honour of it is valued. Haughton fought the stubborn fight from the 3rd to the 15th November, 1841, for his own and other's lives, as stoutly as a man could fight it. He proved the sterling stuff of which he was made. He wanted the Government to recognize it publicly. He got, however, neither a brevet nor a medal. I have known many a man since get a medal without seeing a single shot fired, and without doing one stroke of work for that medal. The man's life, however, is not wasted who has set such an example to the Army, and who gave to India three sons as brave and noble as himself. A man has not served in vain of whom after his death it was written :—

"General Haughton's services were performed in days when there were no special correspondents and no telegraph to India. Men quietly and nobly did their duty, and died, or, if they survived, were not sought out with feverish haste to receive well-earned rewards; and so it is that as brave and noble-minded an officer as ever lived goes to his grave, after performing eminent services in a past generation, with nothing more than a C.S.I. To say that his services were not adequately recognized is saying what may be said of many an old officer who lived and fought in the time when duty, and not decoration, was the order of the day. His life was a great example to those around him, and it may be said of him that he was 'sans peur et sans reproche.'"

The man with such an epitaph was indeed worthy to be the father of the subject of this memoir. Of all the letters which his son John wrote to him, only those from 1880 to 1887 have been preserved, and even of those many are missing; notably all those that followed on the death of Lieut.-Colonel John Haughton's first wife, and all those written during the Delhi camp of exercise of 1885–86. The tone of the son's letters indicate that the most perfect confidence and strongest affection existed between him and his father. I shall have more to say, later on, about these letters, as an index to John Haughton's character and capacities. For the present I will only remark that, in my opinion, the father who received such letters from his son is to be congratulated.

General Haughton had two sons besides John. Richard, the elder, was born at Chyebassa, near Chhota Nagpur, in India, on May 7, 1848. He was educated at Uppingham School, under the Rev. Edward Thring, and at Christ's College, Cambridge, where he took his M.A. degree. After studying medicine for a year or so he gave up a pursuit which he found distasteful, and joining his father in Bengal in 1870, received an assistant-commissionership at Jalpaiguri. Finding that the sedentary employment of the uncovenanted civil service did not suit him, and, preferring a planter's life, he accepted an appointment on a tea plantation in the Darjeeling Terai. While there, an epidemic of cholera broke out. Of his conduct at that time his old friend, Mr. C. Brownfield, thus writes: "He stood undaunted with Archie Campbell, a brother planter, when cholera raged in the tea-gardens, attending to the stricken, the dying, and the dead. The two young planters had themselves to carry the dead and bury them." The staunchness of those two men prevented the entire exodus of the coolies, and thus enabled the work to be carried on. In 1873 he was invited to undertake the management of one or two tea-gardens, but, declining those offers, accepted that of a Dr. Brougham to open up a tea-garden in the Western Dooars or Bhutan Terai. What this district was in 1874, I can best describe in Mr. Brownfield's own words—

"It was a wilderness of unhealthy jungle, a dense growth of vegetation fighting fiercely for the light, vigorous saplings pushing through the leafless branches of giant trees that had been dead for years, and were kept from falling by the creeper cables, which, when in their tender years, clung to the trees for support. A land of prostrating fevers, humid and miasmatic: a luxuriance of foliage above, decayed and decaying wood and leaves below, a land demanding nearly a man's whole energies merely to exist."

Such was the country and climate in which Richard Haughton became the pioneer of a tea-industry which to-day employs thousands of human beings. He was the first man to start a tea-garden there. In four months he succeeded in clearing and planting seventy acres. He also managed, before the rains set in, to build a small two-roomed, earth-floored, mat-walled hut; and thither, in 1874, he brought his wife, the eldest daughter of Captain D. K. Presgrave, and his own first cousin. For twenty-one years Richard Haughton lived and worked in the Western Dooars, opening up, in all, five tea-gardens for Dr. Brougham and two for other employers. He had, unfortunately, bound himself by a promise to Dr. Brougham not to open up tea-gardens on his own account. In return for such an undertaking he, not unnaturally, expected that in due course his employer would take him into partnership. This, however, did not come to pass; and, moreover, during all those twenty-one years he received only eight months' leave. John Haughton's letters from 1880 to 1890 show the anxiety that he felt for his brother Richard's health, doomed as he was to pass the best years of his life in a hotbed of malaria. In 1889 an epidemic of cholera broke out at Soongachi, where one of his tea-plantations lay. After attending the deathbed of a brother planter, and helping the doctor to render the last offices, he was himself seized with the complaint. Fifteen years' familiarity with the fell disease had taught him the best remedies. He applied them promptly and recovered. In 1895 his health completely broke down, and he came home on three months' leave, *grudgingly granted* as it would seem. For the last six years he had been an honorary magistrate of the district, and he was the founder and, while he lived, the honorary secretary of the Dooars Planters' Association. He died in London on May 29, 1895, at the age of forty-seven, and is buried, with two of his children, in Hammersmith Cemetery.

Of the esteem in which he was held by those who knew him best, I have numerous evidences before me. I can but select one or two. One writer says—

"All planters will feel the loss of a most sincere friend, and the district of a man impossible to replace, as very few will exert themselves as he did for the good of the community, and with the truest and most unselfish of motives. He always kept open house, dispensing hospitality with a free hand. What Richard Haughton found a jungle waste now contains eighty-one gardens and 43,600 acres under tea, with the finest appointed bungalows, factories, and machinery of any tea district; and last, not least, the prosperous Bengal Dooars Railway."

Another says—

"His tact, zeal, and energy were crowned with success, for the best things we have achieved here were due either to his initiative or were carried through mainly by his indomitable pluck and perseverance."

The Dooars Planters' Association put his portrait in their club, and a brass tablet to his memory in their church; and to his widow, who had shared his twenty-one years of toil, they gave a still more practical testimonial of their high regard, accompanied by a "resolution" expressing their sincere sympathy with her in her bereavement. The inscription on the tablet is this—

"Erected to the memory of the late Richard Haughton of Soongachi Tea Estate, Jalpaiguri district, who died in London, May 29, 1895, by his planter-friends and others, in recognition of the valuable services he rendered for many years to the tea industry as honorary secretary of the Dooars Planters' Association, and as a mark of the high esteem in which he was held by all who knew him."

Henry Lawrence, the youngest son of General J. C. Haughton, was born at Tavoy on October 1, 1857. He was educated at Winchester and Cambridge. Having passed his "Little Go," he entered the Army in 1878, being posted to the 29th (Worcestershire) Regiment. He volunteered for duty as a Transport-officer in the Afghan campaign, and as such served from October 21, 1879, to May 31, 1881. He accompanied the force, under Major-General Robert Phayre, in its advance to the relief of Kandahar as a Brigade Transport-officer. When the British troops were withdrawn from Kandahar in April, 1881, Henry Haughton returned to India.

CHAPTER III.

JOHN HAUGHTON'S EARLY DAYS.

"Of soldier sire, the soldier son—
Life's honoured eventide
One lives to close in England, one
In maiden battle died."

ARCHBISHOP TRENCH.

JOHN HAUGHTON was born on August 22, 1852, at Chhota Nagpur.

General J. C. Haughton gave his children one name only, except the youngest, who, being born late in 1857, was called Henry Lawrence, after the hero of Lucknow. John, in a letter written to his father in June, 1881, thus comments on his own name, evidently in reply to some remark of his father's—

"John or Jack is all the same to me. My relations may take their choice, but I fear they will not find John a more valuable article than Jack was. As long as they love 'John' none the less than they did 'Jack,' he will be quite content. I am not at all sorry you did not give me a second name. I would not wish for a better than the one I have got, and never have felt any need for a second."

To his relations and best friends he was "Jack" to the end of his life.

Of his childish days there is very little to record. He, like his other brothers and his sister, was sent home to his grandfather (erst professor at Addiscombe) and grandmother at Ramsgate; and was brought up by them, as long as they lived, and, after their death, by General J. C. Haughton's sisters. The only living person who remembers him in childhood is his aunt, Miss Haughton, whose special charge her brother's children were. From what she has written it is evident that he was, as a child, what he was as a man—kind-hearted and tractable, and at the same time resolute and independent. The sands at Ramsgate were his favourite playground, and there he formed friendships with the sailors and fishermen. One very old man was his special favourite, and his big shrimping-net "Jack" might, on occasions, be seen helping to carry home through the crowded streets of Ramsgate. However, enough of childhood's anecdotes. They are at best, as a rule, but childish. His first school was one kept by Miss Wilkes at Canterbury. He was even then growing very rapidly. Later he went to a school at Ramsgate kept by the Rev. A. Manson. In August, 1865, when in his thirteenth year, he was sent to Uppingham, then under the able headmastership of the Rev. Edward Thring. His brother Richard, and two cousins of the name of Rhode, were also at Uppingham, which was then, as now, a school of high repute. Among his contemporaries there were the Rev. Canon Skrine, Warden of Glenalmond, Mr. Maurice Macmillan, Mr. Edward Stanford, and

Colonel J. H. Rosseter, R.A. Among the masters of the school who knew him were the Reverends G. H. Mullins, H. Candler, and E. C. Selwyn, the last-mentioned being now the Headmaster. I am indebted to them and to Mr. Robert Rhode for the little which I have been able to learn of his school-days. His unusual stature was the point that impressed itself on all memories. He was popular with and respected by his schoolfellows. He was not remarkable in any branch of athletics—rapid-growing boys very seldom are,—and that he was not a great scholar is shown by the fact that when he left the school in October, 1868, he was still only in the lower fourth. However, he was educated to go into the Army, and the sterling qualities which he possessed showed themselves in the determined way in which he worked for and gained that end. On leaving Uppingham he was sent to a then well-known "crammer," Dr. Stacpoole of Kingstown near Dublin. When he expressed his intention of going up for the next examination for entrance into Sandhurst, his tutor assured him that he had not the ghost of a chance. Jack Haughton, however, thought otherwise, went up for the examination, and passed, "taking exactly a middle place among the hundred successful candidates." This happened late in 1868 or early in 1869, when he was still well under seventeen years of age. After he left Uppingham he was evidently lost sight of by his school, until in 1897 his name came prominently forward during the

MEMORIAL BRASS IN THE CHAPEL OF UPPINGHAM SCHOOL.

severe fighting in Tirah. Occasionally, if he chanced to be in England, he would attend one of the Old Boys' School Dinners in London. His old form-master, Mr. Candler, in the "In Memoriam" paper which appeared in the June, 1898, number of the *Uppingham School Magazine*, gives these brief reminiscences of him :—

> "He was (as a schoolboy) quiet, gentlemanly, and of good report, and a very pleasant fellow to deal with. . . . I never met my old pupil after he left school, till a few years ago at an Old Boys' School Dinner in London, when he made himself known to me. He was the tallest of the tall, and proportionately well-built, looking every inch a gallant gentleman. His mobile face was full of intelligence and kindness, and it was very pleasant to see him smile. He looked strong and valiant, a man to be depended on and trusted."

How proud his school and schoolfellows were of the distinction he won in Tirah as an able and brave soldier, and of his gallantry in death, I have evidence in letters before me from masters and boys. A movement had already, early in 1898, been started among his old schoolfellows in the Services to put up a memorial to him at Uppingham, when it became known that his brother officers in the 35th and 36th Sikhs proposed to do so. The honour was ceded to them, and in 1899 the brass, reproduced in the accompanying illustration,* was placed in the school chapel.

Of the eighteen months which Haughton spent

* Taken from a photograph by Mr. Stocks of Uppingham.

at Sandhurst, and of the first ten years of his service, scarcely any record is extant, except a very brief memorandum in his own handwriting, written apparently in 1894. I can do no better than quote that.

"From the middle of 1869 until December, 1870, I was at the Royal Military College, Sandhurst. From December, 1870, to October, 1871, I was (with many others) kept waiting for my commission, as the Bill for the abolition of purchase was being considered in Parliament. I was gazetted an ensign in the 1st Battalion 24th Foot (now called South Wales Borderers) on October 28, 1871. I did not purchase my commission, although 'purchase' was not done away with till a few days afterwards. I was one of the last ensigns ever gazetted to the army. The rank of ensign was abolished, if I remember rightly, from November 1, 1871.

"As usual, I did not join the regiment for two months. On January 6, 1872, I sailed from Liverpool. There were on board two other subalterns, Browne and Curteis, to join the 24th Regiment. They had both been at Sandhurst at the same time as myself. Browne gained the V.C. in the Zulu War, and now commands the 2nd Battalion South Wales Borderers. We landed at Malta about January 16, and were there until some time in March, when the regiment proceeded in H.M.'s troopship *Jumna* to Gibraltar. Gibraltar was an expensive place. My father applied for me to be transferred to a regiment in India. I was gazetted to the 72nd Highlanders. I left Gibraltar and the dear old 24th in February, 1874, travelling by P. and O. steamer to Bombay. In those days it took a long time to get through the Canal, so we did as was customary, *i.e.* left the ship (the ill-fated

Bokhara) * at Alexandria, and went by train to Suez, where we embarked on the P. and O. *Pekin.* I may mention that while on board the *Bokhara* we experienced a great gale in the Mediterranean. The ship was overloaded with iron rails and other cargo. The water was several inches deep in the cabins and saloons. We were two days late in the short voyage from Malta to Alexandria. In due course I arrived at Bombay, and proceeded to Peshawur, where the 72nd Highlanders were quartered. I found them a very fine regiment indeed, and have never seen a finer. The officers, too, were pleasant and kindly, although contrary to advice, I let it be known from the first that my final destination must be the Staff Corps.

"At Peshawur we were stationed until the following cold weather, when (about February, 1875, I think) we moved to Nowshera. About May I marched with my company to Attock Fort, and we were there till October. I was then sent to join Regimental Headquarters at Cherat, where they had been during the hot weather. By-the-by when I went to Peshawur, there was no railway beyond Lahore, from which place we went by *dak-gari.*†

"From Cherat I accompanied the Headquarters and right wing to Sialkot. On April 15, 1876, I got six months' leave, and went right down country to stay with my brother Dick, who was a tea-planter at a garden about twenty miles from Jalpaiguri in north-east Bengal. The garden was in what is called the Western Bhutan Dooars. Whilst on leave an order came out that officers from British regiments could be appointed to the Staff Corps, when they had completed one year's service in India, and had passed the lower standard examination in Hindustani. (Previously the qualification was 'two years'

* She went down in a storm in the Straits of Formosa some sixteen years later.

† An Indian method of posting.

service in India, and to have passed the higher standard examination in Hindustani.') Consequently I applied to be appointed to the 10th Bengal Native Infantry, which was then stationed at Jalpaiguri. My reasons for doing so were first to be near my brother, second to escape the expense of the journey back to Sialkot right across India, and thirdly on account of the good *shikar* at Jalpaiguri. I was posted to the 10th Bengal Native Infantry on November 10, 1876; but was at once sent off to Dacca, where there were four companies of the regiment. The usual way to go to Dacca from Jalpaiguri, in those days, was by pony or elephant to Titalia (27 miles), then by *dak-gari* to Sahibganj (100 miles), cross the River Ganges in a steamer, and then by train to Calcutta (about 250 miles). However, having been very 'seedy' with jungle fever, I thought I would like a quieter journey, so hired a country boat—and comfortable enough it was—which, for some sixty rupees, agreed to take me to Dacca. At that season (October) the country is a network of waterways. It only took about eight days to get to Dacca, where I was stationed till the following June. I then went to Calcutta to study Hindustani, and passed the higher standard examination at the beginning of September, 1877. From Calcutta I volunteered for service in the Madras famine.*

* Unfortunately no detailed account is forthcoming of Haughton's work and experiences in this famine, one of the most severe that India has known. Not a single letter to his father of that period is in existence. All that we know is that both for the services he rendered and for the report he sent in, he received the thanks and commendation of the Government of India. His "Record of Service" contains the brief entry, "Employed in Famine Relief Duty in Madras from 21.9.'77 to 10.4.'78, and received the special thanks of the Government of India. G.O.C.C., 21.8.'78, p. 427." Among those thanked in the same resolution (No. 1385, in the P.W.D. of 26.7.'78) is Lieutenant C. H. Des Vœux, the officer who afterwards, as Haughton's second in command, so ably supported him in the defence of the Samana Forts, and in all the hard work and fighting of the Tirah expedition, and who succeeded him in the command of the 36th Sikhs.

"I went by sea to Madras in September, 1877, and was appointed to the Nellore district. I remained there till the following May (1878), and then went back and joined Headquarters of the 10th Bengal Native Infantry at Jalpaiguri. There we remained until the following October, when, in consequence of the Afghan War breaking out, we were suddenly ordered down to Alipore, a suburb of Calcutta. Since my first going to Jalpaiguri the railway there had been made. We remained at Alipore only a month or six weeks, and then were sent to Barrackpore, which is about twelve or fifteen miles from Calcutta. We remained there until about February, 1880, when we were suddenly ordered up to Cachar on account of the Naga War. We went by river-steamer to Calcutta, and then by country boats for two days."

It is from this date that commence the letters from Haughton to his father which have been preserved, and which continue to the time of his father's death in September, 1887. These letters are in themselves evidence of the entire sympathy that existed between the father and the son. When we consider that John Haughton was sent home when little more than an infant, and that "he never saw his father after he was fifteen," * we can only wonder that the tie which bound them together was so strong. It speaks volumes for the manner in which the boy was brought up by his father's sisters, and for the keen interest and

* Letter from Mrs. J. C. Haughton, dated September 5, 1899. When General Haughton came home, in 1873, his son John was at Gibraltar, whence in July, 1874, he went to India, and never returned to England till the spring of 1888, after an absence of more than sixteen years.

sympathetic temperament which empowered the father to exercise, through years of separation, an influence over his children, and to maintain a firm hold on their affection, regard, and trust. John Haughton wrote to him without reserve on all subjects—on his own interests and progress in the Service, on all that concerned his brothers Dick and Harry, on his own views about matters military, social, and political, on his pleasures and anxieties, on his joys and griefs, on the serious and humorous sides of life; and, throughout all he wrote ran a keynote of modesty about himself, kindliness towards others, keen interest in his relations and friends, and strong affection for and confidence in his father.

The earliest letter of his that I have seen, dated February 25, 1880, gives a good picture of the conditions of service in India.

"That very night (Wednesday) a telegram came that we were to leave Barrackpore on Friday morning and embark at Kidderpore on board the s.s. *Sir William Peel.* What with the amount of returns that have to be sent in on such occasions, and what with the sudden mortality among the grandmothers of our servants, which necessitated their immediate return to their homes, we had a pretty lively time of it on Thursday; but, once started and safe on the river, where brigade-majors and other natural foes could not get at us, we commenced a time of great *aram.** We started at daylight on Saturday morning and got as far as Diamond Harbour, where the engines broke down.

* Peace.

By next morning the engines were patched up, and off we started. We can only go in the steamer as far as Balaganj, four days further on; and whether we go on in country boats or march, no one seems to know. In fact, for all that the Calcutta authorities seemed to know about it, Cachar might be in the Arctic Regions.

"*February* 27.—Our engines again broke down.

"*Cachar, March* 21, 1880.—We have not had a very inspiriting time of it here. We were five days in cholera camp, and then moved into the station. Half our men are in tents and are not to be envied. It has rained copiously every day we have been here, and for the last thirty-six hours it has poured. We officers were at first worse off than the men, as the only bungalow we could get into had had the thatch removed. Luckily for us, after four days under umbrellas and waterproof sheets, we got permission to occupy another, and that a waterproof bungalow. Much was our disgust on hearing that we had not come up here for active service, but to 'restore confidence.' No one here ever seems to have lost confidence. The colonel of the 34th Bengal Native Infantry has lost five horses in the last year; so we are sending our horses to Sylhet in the hopes that they may escape the Manipuri disease.

"*March* 23, 1880.—The river has risen twenty-three feet in two days. The tea-planters, after the manner of the British farmer, are grumbling that they are drowned. A fortnight ago they grumbled that they were dried up. It is delightfully cool, but I rather think the planters grumble at that. I am very well but for the most abominable toothache. Our doctor volunteered to pull out the tooth, but after three attempts, each of which seemed nearly to split my head, he only succeeded in breaking a good bit off. Luckily it does not ache much since.

"*March* 26.—Have got a holiday, and am off for three days' shikar."

These casual comments indicate a few of the amenities of Indian service, and of the character and ways of thought and act of the man who wrote them. We must not, however, follow him further through what are, after all, the mere everyday details of an Indian soldier's life. These indicate to some extent why service in India, especially in native regiments, is such an admirable school of training for the British officer. Our army owes more to it than it does to the so-called reforms, *à la Prussienne*, introduced in 1871, or to all the tests that the ingenuity of an era of examinations has been able to invent. The best criticism on the system of theoretical military education, which has been in vogue for the last twenty-eight years, is to be found in the experiences of the Frontier Warfare of 1897, and of the South African Campaign of 1899–1900.

On the return of the 10th Bengal Native Infantry to Calcutta in April, 1880, Haughton tells his father to look out for his home-coming in February, 1884, and speaks of entertaining "faint visions of the Staff College." The "faint vision" faded into nothing; nor need we regret it. The theoretical instruction of our "hothouse for staff officers" would have added little to the splendid natural qualities evinced by him in Tirah. A distinguished general officer, who accompanied the Tirah expedition, writing of Haughton a few weeks after he was killed, spoke of him as "his only hero," and "the finest leader of men" he had ever seen. "Hero" *nascitur, non fit.*

In May, 1880, Haughton got away for three months' shooting in the Terai and Himalayas, where he ultimately joined his brother officer, Major C. H. Palmer, of whom he succinctly remarks, "He and I are great confederates. . . . We always have been the greatest friends." The end of July he spent with his brother Dick at his tea-plantation in the Western Dooars, and early in August he was back at Barrackpore. He concludes his letter of July 20, 1880, to his father, with the following comments, so truly descriptive of the Indian service then as now:—

"When I rejoin, I shall be the only officer at head-quarters, except the Colonel, so shall have enough and to spare of work. This is the irregular system with a vengeance. If they consider the irregular system a good one, they ought to stick to it and not supply us with sufficient red tape to bind the hands and feet of a whole legion of officers. In addition to my own duties as Adjutant and Paymaster, I shall be Quartermaster and Wing Commander, which, in these days, means a considerable amount of office work, and which brings little or no extra pay. To make matters worse, the Ordnance Department have lately exercised their ingenuity in altering all the old 'Forms' and devising many new ones. The long-promised new 'Bengal Army Regulations' have, at last, come out, but before they reached us there were issued many pages of alterations and corrections."

There are certain details of our military system about which we never can say "The old order changeth, yielding place to new." Pluralism is still rife, but a pluralism that benefits the budget, instead of—as of yore—lining the pockets of the favoured myrmidons of monarchs, ministers, and prelates.* Departments are still cunning in the devising of new "Forms." Each new regulation still becomes the parent of a numerous progeny. When a volume of India Army Regulations comes forth to the army, it looks neat and trim in its red attire; but, as year by year it is fed liberally with slips and cuttings from army orders and circulars, the shapely figure grows bulky and unwieldy, and the digestion and assimilation of its contents becomes an almost hopeless task. In this condition, a combined incubus, puzzle, and nightmare to adjutants and staff officers, it remains for years, until, at last, it is "By Order" submitted to a special process of banting in vogue at army headquarters, restored

* "If we take any (native) battalion in the army list at random, we may find as many as twelve or more officers borne on its roll. Of these we may find two to be on furlough, one on leave on medical certificate, two on plague or famine duty, and one, at least, on some temporary employment, not seconded from his regiment. But at any rate, we might say, that leaves six officers for duty (?). Not necessarily. It is seldom that a battalion has not, at least, one officer attending a musketry, transport, signalling, garrison, or equitation class, and, in addition to these, we may find that another officer has been detailed for special duty on reconnaissance, or as an assistant to a recruiting-officer, or for some one of many other possible duties. One way or another it may be confidently asserted that, during a considerable portion of the year, many regiments have only four officers present; but as long as the 'Returns' are correct and up-to-date, that is a matter of small concern to command and district officers. Of these four officers two are probably attached youngsters, who are thus afforded opportunities of masquerading as wing commanders before they have learnt even the minor details of the quartermaster's and transport offices. We know of one battalion in which, of ten officers entitled to special Tirah leave, not one succeeded in getting it, and fifteen days, on a very special occasion, represented the accumulated privilege leave of its officers in 1899."—*Pioneer Mail*, June 1, 1900.

more or less to its pristine shapeliness, and again issued as "a boon and a blessing" to a grateful army.

In his letters at this time John Haughton begins to impress on his father that to enter the Staff Corps is the only course advisable for his younger brother Harry. In this conviction his mind never faltered, and he persevered until he saw "Harry" posted as a probationer to his own corps, the 10th Bengal Native Infantry, in 1881. He was proud of his brother, and of the good reputation that he had brought back from Kandahar as a hard-working and capable officer. He rightly considered that to a man without private means, the Staff Corps affords the most assured livelihood, although he must, from his own experience in the 24th and 72nd, have sympathized with the reluctance that most officers feel in severing themselves for life from regimental service with and command of their own fellow-countrymen. The system under which officers for the Staff Corps are now appointed direct from Sandhurst obviates some of the old difficulties. It has, however, always been felt that a few years' "licking into shape" in a British regiment was a very good training for the candidate for the Staff Corps.

The term "Indian Staff Corps" has had a longer lease of life than most of the names of corps and departments in vogue during the past half century. This is the more noteworthy in that its inception was greeted with keen criticism, and it has not usually been recognized as a really suitable title. If, however, we consider the manner in which this great body of from two to three thousand officers has been employed during the past forty years, not only in regiments and on the army, departmental, and civil staffs, but in every capacity whatsoever, in which Government required their services, we must allow that the name is by no means inappropriate or unhappy. While the numbers of our British regiments have given place to territorial titles, and while the Army Service and Army Medical Corps have several times changed their name and status, the "Indian Staff Corps" changeth not, except in some slight modifications of the conditions of service, promotion, and pension. Although, on its present basis, it can claim a standing of but forty years, it is heir to all the traditions of the East India Company's Native Army from the days of Arcot and Plassy downward. Though the Mutiny transferred the allegiance of this Army from "John Company" to the Crown, and necessitated its thorough reconstitution, nevertheless the glorious victories of the days of Clive, Eyre, Coote, Lawrence, Harris, Baird, Wellesley, Ochterlony, Pollock, and Nott are held to be the heritage of the "Staff Corps" of to-day. Such soldiers as Henry Lawrence, John Nicholson, James Outram, Herbert Edwardes, John Jacob, Henry Norman, Harry Lumsden, Henry Green, Neville Chamberlain, Donald Stewart, Frederick Roberts, Herbert Macpherson, Charles Macgregor, and William

Lockhart are the links that bind the achievements of the first half to the close of the nineteenth century, and interweave the laurels won in Afghanistan (1838–42), the Panjab, Persia, and the Mutiny with those gained later in China, Abyssinia, Burma, Egypt, and Africa (East, Central, and South), and in many a frontier foray and expedition. In the century now about to commence there lies a future before Her Majesty's Indian Army greater than its past, great as that has been. The loyalty of the Native Chiefs has in the last few years won for them a right to participate in the honours of that future. The Imperial Service troops of India are a recognized factor in Imperial defence.*

* The Fourth Brigade sent from India to China in August last, under the command of General Cummins, was largely composed of Imperial Service Troops.

CHAPTER IV.

MARRIAGE AND AFTER.

"Life is mostly froth and bubble;
Two things stand like stone—
Kindness in another's trouble,
Courage in your own."

A. LINDSAY GORDON.

MARRIAGE is bound to exercise a great influence on a man's life. It may not materially alter his character—for character is often too firmly formed before marriage to be altered after it—but it will almost certainly affect his career. Into the life of an Indian soldier it brings many changes, and, unless it be an unhappy marriage, changes for the better. Until he marries, the officer of the Indian army has, as a rule, no home but his regimental mess; and, it is needless to say, that is for most men no home at all. Mess life may suit some men, but to others it is an irksome necessity. Most officers, by the time they reach middle life, are thankful to have homes of their own, in which they are their own masters. No man in a mess is his own master. Besides—to still further regard the matter from a material point of view—the comforts of life in

India are for the benedict and not for the bachelor. Visions of baccalaurean bungalows in bygone days awake few pleasing memories. Over the life which "E. H. A." has so well painted, "Behind the Bungalow," the presiding influence of a memsahib is needed and appreciated.

Such, in brief, is one of the many exoteric points of view of married life in India. Of the esoteric view, of the inner life, every man must speak for himself. No outsider knows that life. When it is unveiled, it comes sometimes as a revelation. Nothing surprised me more, when I read the memories of the "Man of Blood and Iron," than the tenderness and devotion of his letters to his wife. A soft core underlay the adamantine surface. Haughton, too, could be a man of iron, but the outer shell of strong nerve and firm will covered a gentle nature, as his letters, which I shall quote from time to time, will show. Marriage ever involves cares and responsibilities—in India more perhaps than elsewhere—but it brings compensations that far outweigh them.

A letter from John Haughton to his father, dated Barrackpore, February 17, 1881, commences thus—

"No news from you for some mails; neither have I written; my reason being that I have been in a very disturbed state of mind, which you will understand after reading my statement, which perhaps will startle you; but I think if you knew all about it, it would be an agreeable surprise. The fact is I have proposed to and for, and been accepted by Margaretta, third daughter of Mr. E. B. Baker, Deputy Inspector-General of Police;* but the marriage is not to come off for two years, a long, long time."

From the next two or three pages of that letter I shall make no quotations. I consider that these confidences are private—not suited for biographies. Suffice it to say that all he wrote there does honour to the lady he selected for his wife, and honour to his own head and heart; and, after all, it filled less than a sheet, and concluded with the wise words—

"Now I've told you all. I know from experience that engaged men often are great bores, so I won't bore you any more at present. I shall very anxiously await a letter from you after your receipt of this."

Passing from domestic to regimental affairs, he says—

"Our re-organization has commenced with a vengeance, for have we not been ordered to get a new pattern forage-cap, new badges of rank, and new shoulder-cords? I used to wear crowns on my collar, now every garment is to have a star over each shoulder-cord. These excrescences on the shoulders are not becoming; but what are appearances when the efficiency of the army is at stake? It only costs each officer about £10, which of course is nothing with so great an object in view."†

* A brother of his, Colonel Charles Baker, V.C., was very well known as chief of the police in Egypt in succession to Colonel Valentine Baker. He had previously commanded Rattray's Sikhs, when it was still a police battalion.

† A few months later Haughton writes to his father that he

In March, 1881, Haughton's regiment was moved to Benares, and his letters now first introduce us to a very remarkable old lady, Mrs. Kennedy, who then lived there. When the Prince of Wales was in India, in 1876, he called upon her, for he wished to see and pay a compliment to one who had passed in India a life, in length far beyond the ordinary span, and who by her own personality and by her connections and associations was a woman of mark. Her activity and vitality, moreover, at an age verging on a hundred, were such as are rarely seen. Her husband had died about 1858. He had then seen sixty-two years' service and was commanding a division. The General Capsicum to whom Captain Bellew's "Memoirs of a Griffin" introduces us at Calcutta, would seem to have belonged to a similar school—a school that died out after the Mutiny. At the time of her husband's death, Mrs. Kennedy had been married fifty-five years. She lived for twenty-seven years after his death; she was married, therefore, in 1802. Up to 1881 she always went to church twice every Sunday, but in 1882 she consented to go once only, though she always stood and knelt with the rest of the congregation. She was to the last in possession of every faculty. She had evidently been an old friend of General J. C. Haughton, for his son John often mentions her in writing to his father, speaks of his kind reception

desires to pay off all debts before marriage, and that his total debts amount to Rs. 1300, "mostly due to my military tailor for changes in uniform."

by her on his first visit to her in March, 1881, and in July of that year remarks—

"Mrs. Kennedy is as active as ever still, though I hear that she admits that she must be getting old, now that she has a grandson a brigadier-general, whom she considers 'a very lucky *young* fellow.'" *

In April, 1884, she thought of undergoing an operation for cataract, but probably it was not performed. This venerable and very highly respected lady passed away at the end of October, 1884. Haughton thus writes to his father of the event on November 4—

"Dear, kind old Mrs. Kennedy has succumbed to that attack of bronchitis. She died on Saturday and was buried on Sunday, every European and the leading natives, headed by the Maharaja (of Benares), attending her funeral. Almost the last coherent words she spoke were some verses from the 23rd Psalm."

The loss which the army has recently sustained in the death of Field-Marshal Sir Donald Stewart, induces me to quote here some of the remarks on him which I find in Haughton's letters to his father. Those letters were written, be it remembered, in perfect frankness and sincerity. There are circumstances under which the candid utterances of a subaltern may outweigh the calculated praises of more prominent eulogists. In one letter, written towards the close of 1880, Haughton discusses at some length—evidently in reply to inquiries made

* Brigadier-General T. G. Kennedy, C.B., Commandant of the Panjab Frontier Force.

by his father—the conduct of the military operations in Afghanistan, and the generalship displayed. The points about Sir Donald Stewart that struck him were these: the quiet thoroughness, devoid of all show, with which he carried out all his duties as General-in-Chief in Afghanistan; his determination to be obeyed; the high respect all entertained for him; and the magnanimity which prompted him to give Sir Frederick Roberts 10,000 of his picked troops and his best transport and send him to relieve Kandahar, while he reserved for himself the more onerous but less showy task of withdrawing the troops from Kabul to Peshawar.

To the timely reforms which Sir Donald, as Commander-in-Chief, sought to introduce into the Army in India, Haughton in several letters refers appreciatively. In a letter dated June 26, 1881, the following passage occurs:—

"The Army has great faith in our new Chief, Sir Donald Stewart, and, judging by one or two cases that have occurred, he does not intend that regimental officers and soldiers proper should be the sport and plaything of departments and clerks, as they have been for years. The way the Pay, Ordnance, Commissariat, and other Departments were allowed to harass the regimental folk was most vexatious. We have lately had two skirmishes, one with the Pay and the other with the Musketry Departments, and, thanks to Sir Donald, have triumphed in both. Another good point in Sir Donald is that he is, apparently, not going to endorse the old saying 'once on the Staff, always on the Staff,' and is sending men to regimental duty on the completion of their five years' tenure of office.

So, please goodness, we shall be no more bullied by D.A.A.G.'s, etc., who have never done a stroke of regimental work since they were subalterns, and then, as often as not, were given a staff appointment as a sort of dowry with their wives."

Later on, in 1881, Haughton condemns the heedless way in which district and other staff officers, who receive regular weekly returns from corps, nevertheless invariably telegraph for every detail or statistic they may want, thereby greatly and needlessly increasing correspondence. In October, 1882, he says—

"It appears to me that all Government servants are hampered from doing their really important work by the amount of useless writing they have to do. I rejoice to say that since Sir Donald Stewart has been chief, the pruning-knife has been at work, and has considerably reduced the number of returns."

Haughton's letters contain, not unnaturally, a number of comments on the conduct of the Afghan campaign of 1878–81. Although most of them are sound and true, I do not see that any good purpose is served by repeating them here. I will make one exception, and that because the opinion expressed contradicts the common version. After the battle of Maiwand, and, what was far worse, the incapacity displayed at Kandahar, the Press of Upper India commenced a tirade against the Bombay Native Army, somewhat analogous to the "stupidity of the British officer" cry raised by the *Times* after the Koornspruit affair. For the moment the passion of criticism obscured judgment. It did not trouble itself about facts or accurate knowledge. The writers, like many of the war correspondents and critics of to-day, knew little of military history, either in or out of India, and probably nothing of the history of the army that they criticized with such confidence. The Bombay Native Army has a record of which it is justly proud. The calm and unbiassed testimony of a Bengal officer to the gallant bearing of the two Bombay infantry regiments at Maiwand is worth more than the heated criticism of journalists, some of whom got no nearer the scene of action than Kandahar. The passage I would quote occurs in a letter dated towards the end of 1881. It is this:—

"I had a talk the other day with a man who had visited the Maiwand battlefield. He says that the Bombay Grenadiers must have fought grandly, as evinced by the marks of slaughter and the empty cartridges where they stood *firm in their ranks.** The 66th were not much under fire (as the Grenadiers and Jacob's Rifles were), until the fatal break when they may have been partly carried away by the repulsed Jacob's Rifles.† Bodies of the 66th stood nobly later on to the last man."

* I traversed in January, 1881, this line of cartridge-cases from where Jacob's Rifles had fought on the left to the depression occupied by the 66th on the right. All the infantry stood "firm in their ranks" for at least four hours.—A. C. Y.

† Of the seven British officers who went into action with Jacob's Rifles, two were killed, one had a leg taken off by a round shot, and three were more or less severely wounded. All the native officers with the companies on the extreme left of Burrows' line were killed or wounded. These companies only fell back when the battery supporting them ran out of ammunition and was withdrawn.—A. C. Y.

In the autumn of 1881 Harry Haughton came from his regiment (29th Foot) at Mhow, on a visit to his brother John at Benares, and accompanied him to Darjiling, where Mrs. Baker and her daughters Margaretta (John's *fiancée*) and Flora were spending the hot weather. Before Harry's leave was over, he had become engaged to Miss Flora Baker. This, at any rate, decided the question which John had been so long advocating, viz. Harry's transfer to the Staff Corps. The only possible way to matrimony lay through the Staff Corps, and that by accepting employ in the Pay, Commissariat, or Transport Departments—to all intents and purposes the life of a civilian, gilded with extra pay and military titles. All plans for the future were, however, cut short by Harry's death of cholera in July, 1882, at Benares. John, who had been caused much anxiety during the past eighteen months by the delicate health of his *fiancée*, had gone, on July 6, from Benares to Barrackpore, on ten days' leave to see her. He was recalled to Benares a few days later by a telegram announcing his brother's seizure by cholera. In his letter, dated July 13, he tells all to his father.

"I trust my telegram to uncle Hannyngton will have broken to you the sad news of my dear brother Harry's death, and I pray to God that He may have given you strength and comfort. The poor boy died of cholera at half-past eight on Sunday evening, and was buried in the cemetery here next day. On the previous Wednesday (July 5) he returned from a ten days' trip to Barrackpore, and was then apparently well. On Thursday (6th) morning I went away to Barrackpore, and never saw him again. My dear comrade and friend, Major Palmer, did all that a brother could have done both for him and me. From what Major Palmer tells me, and from the dear boy's own letters, it appears that on Thursday evening, when Major Palmer was driving him up from the library, he complained of being very sick, and felt very ill for about three hours, with what was supposed to be a bad bilious attack. On Friday and Saturday he went about much as usual, except that he said he did not feel strong enough to play tennis. On Sunday (July 9) he wrote that he was better though still very weak. He was taken ill about eleven o'clock in the day, and died quite peacefully at 8.30 in the evening from weakness. Major Palmer telegraphed to me on Sunday afternoon. I started by the next train, which left on Monday morning, but did not hear the sad news till I reached Moghal Serai. It grieves me most to think of you, dear father. In the few months we have been together I have learnt to love him very dearly, and to know what a gentle, loving disposition was his. I know from his own lips that Flora Baker's love not only made his last year on earth a very happy one, but made him more fit for the life to come, and may God bless her for it. I hope I have done right in telegraphing to General Hannyngton. I cannot write more now."

Harry Haughton had won the esteem and regard of his brother officers of the 29th Foot. So much so, that Colonel Ruxton of that regiment wrote to John Haughton and said that it was the wish of the officers of the 29th to put up a monument to him. John, writing to his father on July 23, says—

"It grieves me to think we shall never see dear Harry again, but that is our loss. I have kind friends here to whom I owe much gratitude, most of all to Major Palmer. I have received many kind letters, especially one from Major Watson of the 29th, who says, speaking of you, 'When you are writing home, will you kindly express our deep sympathy with him in the loss he has experienced, and let him know how much we valued and esteemed his son.' Words of themselves are not of much value, but the sympathy of real friends is an honour to the memory of those who are gone, and I value it much."

Again, on December 19, 1882, John writes to his father—

"I have had a letter from Colonel Ruxton of the 29th, advising me of the completion of the monument they wish to erect over our dear Harry's grave. I think it is a well-chosen one—a plain marble cross on a marble base, with the inscription, 'Erected by his brother officers to Lieutenant Henry Lawrence Haughton, of the 1st Battalion Worcester Regiment. Born October 1, 1857; died July 6, 1882.'"

On January 18, 1883, at 3.45 p.m., John Haughton was married at St. Bartholomew's Church at Barrackpore to Margaretta Louisa Baker. By the evening of the 24th, Haughton and his wife had arrived at Benares, and there they remained until the sad event in October which brought their brief married life to a close. In the summer of 1883 we find John strongly urging his father and stepmother to come out to India the next cold weather, and join him and his wife during the summer of 1884 in a trip to Kashmir. Any such project as this, however, passed into oblivion amid the grief that ensued on the death of his wife at Benares. His son (christened Henry Lawrence, after his youngest brother) was born on November 1. The mother died on November 8. How deeply Haughton felt this loss, those who knew him best, know best. His friend Major Gunning Hunter, of the 10th Jats (quondam 10th Bengal Native Infantry), writing to me in March, 1899, says—

> "There is no doubt that his wife's death affected the whole of his after life; but he had a wonderful silent self-control. Directly she died, he plunged into a study of military matters. He got books he never thought of, I am sure, before, and used to work at them, and argue over them. The first motive was, I think, to draw off his mind from his trouble; and from that he got more and more keen. Not, mind, that he was not always keen—only, he never went ahead like that before. It was the Delhi camp of 1885–86 that brought Haughton to the front. Though Tirah was the first (and last) active service that he saw, every one knows that few men *knew* more of active service. He was a man of men, 'sans peur et sans reproche.'"

Haughton's little boy was confided to the care of his maternal grandmother, who came from Calcutta to Benares to look after him, when he was left motherless.

John Haughton had always been a keen soldier, taking an intelligent interest in all that concerned his profession. After the loss of his wife, he turned his attention more closely to the study of his profession. He also returned to his chummery with his friend Major Palmer. His letters to his father in 1884 are very much occupied with the infant "Henry Lawrence," which is but natural. 1884 was also the era of the dynamitard in England, and elicits this comment from Haughton—

> "It is intolerable that England should be oppressed by a comparatively small body of fiends. If one wants to lead a quiet life, the only chance will be to flee to the most uncivilized region possible; and it seems a question whether oppression by the ruling classes, as in Turkey, will not soon be preferable to oppression by the discontented refuse of humanity in more civilized parts."

This view of matters may not have occurred to the ardent advocates of Armenian emancipation. We often fail to see the beam in our own eye. Recent assassinations or attempted assassinations of royal personages add point to this remark. All Europe is now "oppressed by a comparatively small body of fiends," with which modern law and justice is too feeble to cope. The humanity of to-day bids us coddle and conciliate the criminal.

It was about this time, also, that the controversy regarding the respective value of old and young soldiers was going on. In Haughton's letter to his father of April 1, 1884, is the following remark: "The *Pioneer* says of our three Generals, 'One likes to fight with very young soldiers, the second likes old soldiers, the third likes to fight his battles without any soldiers at all.'"* Apropos of this,

* The three Generals are Viscount Wolseley, Lord (then Sir Frederick) Roberts, and Charles (*alias* "Chinese") Gordon.

it is worthy of note that Sir Harry Lumsden of the Guides, who had seen as much stern fighting as most men, was of opinion (as his biographers relate) that, if a tough bit of work had to be done, young soldiers were the best to do it. He concluded that they in their inexperience knew not danger or fear. On the other hand, the term "veteran troops" is one that is synonymous with "troops fit for any emprise." In the present war with the Boers, our young short-service soldiers, well leavened with Reservists, have done splendidly. If the respective merits of the young and old soldier is matter for controversy, the South African War can only decide that the young ones are worthy to tread in the footsteps of the old—and they can have no higher praise. For faults of training and organization the soldier is not responsible.

July and August of 1884 Haughton spent at Raniket, where his mother-in-law, sister-in-law, and infant son were spending the hot weather. This year (1884) was, as I judge by a careful perusal of his letters to his father, the turning-point in his career, the flood of the tide, when the wave of destiny, at first threatening in its aspect, took him up on its crest and bore him through thirteen years of the storms and lulls, ups and downs of service, during the last months of which he faced danger and defied death and defeat, to that final hour when he gave himself to save others, and so brought the bark of his life gallantly, with colours nailed to the mast, into the haven of rest. A fact, full of pathos, has very lately come to my knowledge, and I venture, in all sympathy with those whom it most deeply affects, to mention it here. One of the Commandants under whom John Haughton served in the 10th Bengal Native Infantry, was Colonel Firth. Shortly after the sad news of Haughton's death arrived, he wrote to Colonel C. H. Palmer, the brother officer and most intimate friend of both: "The best thing I could wish for my boy is that he should follow Haughton's example and, if need be, die like him." Colonel (now Major-General) Firth's only son has very recently died at Bloemfontein, having served honourably in "The Buffs" under Lord Roberts in all the marching and fighting that resulted in the relief of Kimberley, the surrender of Cronje at Paardeberg, and the occupation of Bloemfontein.

It was in 1884 that John Haughton became personally known to Sir Herbert Macpherson, a General Officer, whose reputation at that time was second only to that of Sir Donald Stewart and Sir Frederick Roberts. It was undoubtedly owing to this that, in November, 1885, he, to his surprise, found himself appointed to be a Brigade-Major at the Ambala-Delhi Camp of Exercise, the most important manœuvres ever held in India, and which were attended by military officers deputed by the chief Continental powers of Europe, by the United States, and by Japan.

It will be remembered that when, in April, 1885,

war with Russia appeared to be imminent, the Government of India was found to be in a most unprepared state for war. It was almost as unprepared as that of Russia. For this the Empire was indebted to the policy which had not only withdrawn our troops in April, 1881, from Kandahar, but, what was still worse, had suspended the construction of the railway from Sibi to Quetta. Had Quetta and the Kozhak Pass been then connected by rail with India, the attitude of our Government towards that of Russia over the Panjdeh affair ought to have been very different from what it actually was. Whether the Amir Abdurrahman really pronounced himself unwilling to go to war for "that strip of desert" (Badghis), or whether he was induced to adopt that opinion, matters little now. Suffice it that that was the view acted upon; and, as a consequence, we have now a Russian railway, Russian troops, and Russian siege artillery within seventy miles of Herat; while the Russians entertain themselves, and exercise the Amir, by experiments in mobilization on the frontier contiguous thereto. There is little in connection with the settlement of the Russo-Afghan frontier from Zulfikar to Khamiab to which we can now look back with any feeling of satisfaction. The official policy of the hour was a pusillanimous one. It had Afghans and Turkomans, supported by five hundred picked Indian troops under thirty British officers, on the spot, to protect British and Afghan interests. It had thousands of Tekes ready to rise in revolt in rear of the Russians. All this power was neglected. Tall talk and concession were the keynotes of our policy. This train of thought has been suggested by somewhat similar reflections made by Haughton in his letters at this period to his father. As one who was with the Afghan Boundary Commission from September, 1884, to June, 1885, I am in full sympathy with his views. Haughton, writing a fortnight before the affair of Panjdeh, expresses surprise that the Government still declines to push the railway beyond Sibi. No one who now looks back on the events of that time need feel any surprise. The more intimately he was associated with those events, the more keenly will he feel the disappointment of lost possibilities. In the same letter, Haughton writes—

"Reports state that Lumsden, with our Commission, has gone into Persian territory. Such a proceeding must damage our prestige, if true. I should imagine, with the Afghans on our side, and having with him four hundred of the pick of our native army and a very large number of officers, he ought to be able to defend Herat for months against anything the Russians can bring against it for the present. Of course war with Russia is not to be entered on with French gaiety or light heartedness (light-headedness?), but giving in to Russians is not the way to avoid war, and I notice signs of giving in. A few days ago the Russians had entered 'Afghan territory,' now Mr. Gladstone tells us they are 'on debateable ground.'"

There can be no question that had the unprovoked Russian attack at Panjdeh resulted in war between Great Britain and Russia, it would have been the duty of Sir Peter Lumsden and his escort to have marched into Herat and aided the Afghans in its defence. As the correspondent of the *Pioneer* at the time with the Afghan Boundary Commission, I remember writing very strongly on the point; but I had a grave apprehension in my mind that, should war break out, the Commission would have been *ordered* to move into Persia. I feel almost thankful that the issue was never put to the test. To have seen thirty British officers and five hundred good sabres and bayonets marched into Persia, while the defence of Herat was left to our allies the Afghans, would have been too humiliating. The shades of Eldred Pottinger would have haunted us. The mistake made was in moving our escort of five hundred back to Gulran, instead of encamping it at Panjdeh. Its presence there was a duty that we owed to ourselves and to the Amir. The "Panjdeh affair" is one of those incidents in history to which we can only look back regretfully as a "lost opportunity." The part played by Sir Robert Phayre's Division in the relief of Kandahar in August, 1880, suggests similar reflections. I have always felt that if the days that were wasted near the Kozhak Pass had been employed in pushing on to Kandahar, the Bombay Division might have achieved, or at least shared, the honour which fell to the force sent from Kabul.

CHAPTER V.

PREFERMENT.

"Fool not, for all may have,
If they dare try, a glorious life or grave."
GEORGE HERBERT.

IN the spring of 1885 Haughton decided that it was time to send his little son, who was eighteen months old, home to his father's house. For some years past the health of his father had been to him a growing anxiety, as frequent allusions in his letters show. The same letters reveal the great strength of his affection for and pride in his boy. With that frankness and that confidence in his father's sympathy which always evinced itself in his letters, he wrote freely to him about his child. Once his son had gone home, his thoughts were there with him. He himself had never visited England since January, 1872. He was not, however, despite his wish, destined to see England for some years to come—not, unfortunately, until after his father's death.

In a letter dated "Banda, October 24, 1885," we find the germ of the idea which gave him that opportunity which he needed for showing the splendid qualities he possessed as a soldier and as a leader of men. He writes—

"We are in an uncomfortable state of uncertainty, as numerous changes in the native army are, I believe, imminent. It is announced that we are to be formed in regiments of three battalions, and it is possible our system of promotion will be altered. Then there are several new regiments to be raised. I should much like to be appointed to one of the new Sikh regiments, but do not see any hope of it; and, in any case, shall not apply unless names are called for."

On November 3, he writes—

"These splendid accounts of the little Harry keep me in first-rate spirits. He is now two years old, and I have indeed great cause to be thankful for the uninterrupted course of health and strength and progress he has had. Before going further I must tell you the last bit of news, which is, that I am going to the great camp of exercise in the capacity of Brigade-Major of the 1st Brigade, 2nd Division, of the Northern Force. I was struck all of a heap when I saw it in the paper this morning, and hardly believed it, until I saw it confirmed in general orders. Of course I ought to be and am very thankful, both for the honour of being selected and for the chance of its opening the way to a permanent appointment some day. But I cannot help feeling very nervous. I have never had any experience of a Brigade-Major's work, nor of a camp of exercise in any capacity, nor of active service in any capacity; so I can only hope to make up for want of experience by hard work and willing heart. But I cannot help feeling that it is very lucky for the Brigade that it is only a camp of exercise and not real service. I do not imagine we get any pay, and fear it will be rather expensive; but, if I can pass the ordeal successfully, it will have been a grand thing for me, both for the insight into the work of Brigade-Major, and also in many other ways, not the least being the opportunity I shall have of studying the ways of other native regiments, and picking up hints and wrinkles therefrom."

Such is the spirit in which John Haughton, the young captain who afterwards became the hero of the Tirah campaign, welcomed his first nomination to a staff appointment—temporary, it is true, but a greater test of a soldier's worth as a staff officer in the field than all the clerical work at Army, Divisional, or Brigade Headquarters. For the last few years incessant warfare of the pen has raged in the Indian and also in the home papers as to the respective merits of the "P.S.C." and "Non.-P.S.C." officer. Haughton was not a Staff College man. The spirit that worked in him was not born of any "curriculum." The Staff College cannot make a good soldier out of a man devoid of soldierly instinct or talent; but given the groundwork of instinct and talent, it can temper it by training, and improve it by knowledge. The "coping-stone" is practical experience. Add to these a heart in the right place, as that of Haughton certainly was, and we have the beau-ideal of the staff officer. Their number is extremely limited. Haughton's only other staff appointment was a brief tenure of a staff captaincy in the Intelligence Division of the War Office. He found the atmosphere of the establishment uncongenial to him, and resigned the post. Clerical work after all was not the sphere of his abilities. Despite all the talk about and craving after staff employ, there is no finer field for an officer than regimental work. The finest generals and best leaders of troops come from the ranks, not of the staff, but of the regimental officers. Haughton was a splendid regimental officer, and a good staff officer for field work. He was not a clerk, though, as a regimental or brigade staff officer, he did his clerical work carefully, conscientiously, and accurately.

At the end of his letter of November 3, Haughton adds—

"There are pages and pages of General orders about this camp of exercise which I must study carefully, besides many other things, to try and make myself fit for the trial. Mine is a fine Brigade, consisting of the 14th and 96th Foot, the 14th Sikhs, and the 1st Sikhs (of the Panjab Frontier Force)."

On November 10, he writes—

"I am doing my best to make myself acquainted with my duties as Brigade-Major, and I find that with my lack of experience I shall have a lot to remember. . . . The two (Ambala and Delhi) forces when together will number close on forty thousand fighting men, and are composed almost entirely of the troops which were to have gone to meet the Russians in case of war; though in that case they would have had older and more experienced staff officers, and I should have been out of it."

The officer who was appointed to the command of the 1st Brigade, 2nd Division, Northern Force, was Colonel G. B. Wolseley, brother of Viscount Wolseley, and now Lieut.-General Sir George Wolseley, Commanding the Forces in Madras. It is curious that not a single letter written by Haughton to his father between November 10, 1885, and May 22, 1886, is now forthcoming. I am therefore unable to give any account of these manœuvres—the most interesting ever held in India—from Haughton's pen. I was myself there, as Brigade and afterwards Divisional Transport Officer; but I did not come in contact with Haughton. I know, however, from the letters of Colonel C. H. Palmer and Major Gunning Hunter, that Haughton had won golden opinions from his Brigadier. I therefore decided to write to the latter direct, and in August, 1898, received the following reply:—

"Woodside, Ootacamund, August 10, 1898.

"DEAR MAJOR YATE,

"Pray excuse the delay in replying to your note of May 28, which reached me whilst out shooting. I had not lost sight of it—and since my return I have been hunting everywhere for the diary kept either by John Haughton himself, or my orderly officer, during the camp of exercise, 1885–86. As yet I have been unsuccessful, and only yesterday I went carefully through a box of papers which I thought contained the Journal. If I find it, I shall do what you ask me. Yes, I was certainly the first who brought poor Haughton to notice; and the Adjutant-General's office at Simla can doubtless give you a copy of my report on him after the camp broke up. It was, I know, to the effect that Haughton was an exceptionally good staff officer, and one whom it would be to the best interests of our Army in India to push to the front. He had lost his first wife not long before I became associated with him at Delhi; so he was somewhat down in his luck at that time. Still he was always a genial, pleasant member of our little mess, and when I had ladies in my camp for the big march past, he was a great favourite with all. His great characteristics as a soldier were his keenness and reliability. I learned before he had been many days with me that I could thoroughly depend upon any information that he gave me. That is a *sine-qua-non*, in my opinion, in all staff officers. Then his tact and judgment in dealing with commanding officers, and his nice manner with all, impressed me most favourably. In fact, I well remember feeling that he was just the man I should like to have with me on service; and his deplorable death and previous good work in the late campaign proved how just my estimate of him was. If I can only find my 1885–86 diary, I shall write again.

"Meanwhile believe me, truly yours,

"G. B. WOLSELEY."

An application which I made to the Adjutant-General's office at Simla was, however, unsuccessful in eliciting any trace of Colonel G. B. Wolseley's report on Captain J. Haughton. We need, however, no higher testimony than the kind-hearted letter I have just quoted. That Haughton's conduct of his duties at the Ambala-Delhi manœuvres won for him the approval of the authorities is proved by subsequent events. All eye-witnesses of the march-past at Delhi early in February (1886) will recall the pouring rain in which it took place—and through which the Viceroy (the Marquis of

Dufferin and Ava) and the Commander-in-Chief sat on horseback unflinchingly—as also the terrible state of the ground. It became, after the artillery and cavalry had passed over it, ankle-deep in mud. It struck me then, and has recurred to me often since, that a prescient Staff would have made the infantry march past just outside the line which the artillery and cavalry had ploughed up. They would still have been within a reasonable distance of the Viceroy and Commander-in-Chief—a distance at which they could be well seen, and from which they could salute without loss of effect. As it was, however, they were left to plough through the mud. Every good battalion, of course, braced itself for the occasion; and indeed the admirable steadiness with which some battalions, notably the Highland Light Infantry, went by, elicited from the spectators loud marks of approval. There were, it is true, exceptions; but in passing judgment on them we must remember that in such mud the native shoe must come off. One regiment was very severely and deservedly censured for falling into an unseemly and unsoldierly state of disorder on this occasion. Possibly some of that censure might have been appropriately transferred to the Staff which failed to rise to the occasion, and left the troops to worry through the mire as best they could.

On June 12, 1886, Haughton writes home thus:—

"I told you last week about my appointment to the

39th Bengal Infantry.* I have since received the official order, so it is all right, and I shall probably start on Monday night for Cawnpore. I had a letter a short time since from Colonel Wolseley, who was my Brigadier at the camp. He very kindly asked me to come and stay with him at Dalhousie. He also enclosed the copy of a letter he had sent to the Military Secretary to the Commander-in-Chief, asking that I might be appointed to the Brigade Majorship at Sialkot, which will shortly be vacant, and recommending me for it in the most flattering terms. Of course it is most gratifying to me to know that I performed my duties at the camp to his satisfaction, but the authorities, having just given me this promotion (a wing command in the 39th Bengal Infantry), are not likely to give me a staff appointment just now. I am afraid that they may think that I have been trying to 'work the oracle,' but the request on Colonel Wolseley's part was quite spontaneous and voluntary. I have not asked for anything, and do not intend to. What a change in one's prospects a single day brings forth—from seventh in a

* Extract from Regimental Orders by Lieut.-Colonel C. H. Palmer, Officiating Commandant 10th Bengal Infantry. 668

C.O.'s order on Captain Haughton's transfer.

'Thursday, June 10, 1886.

"With reference to regimental order No. 663, of June 9, 1886, Lieut.-Colonel C. H. Palmer, Officiating Commandant, cannot permit Captain J. Haughton, who has been with the regiment nearly ten years, to leave it without hereby placing on record his very high opinion of his character and his qualifications as an officer, and his esteem for him as a friend and a brother officer. In losing Captain Haughton the regiment loses an officer who has always had its interests closely at heart, and one who has effectively done everything in his power to uphold its good name, and Lieut.-Colonel Palmer feels sure he only expresses, in the above remarks, the feelings of all ranks in the corps, and that all with him congratulate Captain Haughton on his promotion in the 39th Regiment Bengal Infantry, and that their best wishes for his welfare go with him.

"J. GUNNING HUNTER, Lieutenant,
"Adjutant 10th Bengal Infantry."

regiment to being third, and to a position of responsibility." *

In March, 1887, the 10th Bengal Infantry being ordered on active service in Burma, Captain Haughton offered to resign his wing in the 39th and rejoin the 10th. The Commander-in-Chief did not accept the offer, but very shortly afterwards appointed him to a permanent wing in the 35th Sikhs, which was now ordered to be raised. On May 12 Captain Haughton wrote—

"The 35th is to be raised at Ferozpur, and is to be composed entirely of 'Jat' Sikhs from north of the Sutlej. They are the very best class of Sikhs. I believe the usual rule about not being able to take leave until one has been ten months in an appointment, will not apply in my case, as I have been in a cognate appointment; but my leave will probably be delayed two or three months. That is a sore disappointment to me, and will be so, I fear, to my dear old father; but it would have been professional suicide to have declined the appointment which, please remember, I never applied for."

His letters for the next few months show that the news he received of his father's health was anything but good, and indicate the anxiety and apprehension he felt that he might not see him again.† He chafed under the obligation which forced him to stay with his new corps until the recruiting and training of it was advanced somewhat. "Just at

* The 39th Bengal Infantry was then the "Allygarh regiment." It is now the "39th Garhwalis."

† General J. C. Haughton had a serious fall in the streets of Paris in January or February of 1887.

present what spare time I have," he writes in July from Ferozpur, "is taken up with Panjabi and books relating to the Sikhs."

His father to the last retained his keenness to learn anything he could about the Gurkhas who escaped from the siege and massacre of Charikar and who settled in its neighbourhood. On July 30, 1887, his son writes thus from Ferozpur—

"One officer in this regiment (35th Sikhs) says he saw one of your Gurkhas at Siah Sang. He had, of course, become a Mohammedan, and appeared to be tolerably well-off. This officer also saw, at Tangi Wardak in Maidan, on the road to Ghazni, an Englishman who stated he had been a soldier in a British regiment, and that he had been left behind wounded in January, 1842, and had been taken care of by an Afghan whose daughter he had subsequently married. Of course he had turned Mussulman. He had almost forgotten English. He said he was well-off and happy and had no wish to leave the country. I am on the track of an officer of the 4th Gurkhas, who, I am told, had a long conversation with the quondam Gurkha."

In the latter part of July, 1887, Haughton was at Amritsar on recruiting duty. By September the 35th Sikhs had been recruited up to the full strength of 912 of all ranks. On September 19 telegraphic news of his father's death reached John Haughton. His letter, expressive of his sense of his own loss and of his sympathy for his step-mother, is such as might be expected from one with so kind and true a heart, and such strong religious convictions. With his sympathy is mingled deep regret that his father should have been taken away within a few months of the time when he himself confidently looked forward to obtaining two years' leave home, and a strong tendency, however uncalled for, to reproach himself for not having gone home earlier, and so seen his father before his death. (He had never seen him since 1867, when he was fifteen years old.) It was on April 14 of the following year (1888) that he landed in England after sixteen years' absence. It is evident that he soon afterwards turned his attention to the study of the Russian language, for, on February 20, 1889, he writes from St. Petersburg, whither, after passing the preliminary examination, he had gone to read for the interpretership. Three letters, of no great interest or importance, are the only relics of his residence in St. Petersburg.

In August, 1890, he returned to England, qualified as an interpreter in Russian, and was offered the post of Staff-Captain in the Intelligence Division of the War Office in succession to Major A. F. Barrow. During the autumn of that year I myself visited Russia and, subsequently, Trans-Caspia and Turkistan. On my return thence I made the acquaintance of Captain J. Haughton, whom I found employed in the Intelligence Division of the War Office. He did not stay there long. In August, 1891, he sent in his resignation, and early in 1892 returned to India and rejoined his appointment as wing commander in the 35th Sikhs. On October 29, 1891, he had attained the rank of Major.

Lieut. Craster. Lieut. Browne. 2nd Lieut. Van Someren.

Lieut. Munn. Capt. Custance. Capt. Prall, I.M.S. Col. Haughton. Lieut. Turing. Major Des Vœux. Capt. Searle.

OFFICERS OF THE 36TH SIKHS. TIRAH, 1897.

(*Taken at Karappa Camp, Oct. 27, 1897.*)

The period of John Haughton's life on which I am now entering is, strange to say, the one of which I have fewest records. Not a single letter of his of this period has come into my hands. He at once, on rejoining, assumed the duties of Officiating Second-in-Command, and on April 20, 1893, was made permanent in that appointment. On April 15, 1893, he became Officiating Commandant, during the absence of Colonel Goldney on leave. On June 25, 1894, he was appointed Commandant of the 36th Sikhs, having then less than twenty-three years' service. His promotion had been unusually rapid, for the Bengal Army. On September 18, 1894, he was married at Durham to Miss Helen Barmby, daughter of the Rev. J. Barmby, D.D., Rector of Pittington, near Durham. He and his wife left England for India on October 12, and, after a brief visit to Nowgong, went on to Ambala. There he rejoined the 36th Sikhs, the regiment in command of which he was destined to do such splendid service. After spending a week at a Darbar camp at Lahore, Major Haughton marched with his regiment to Bannu. His late Commandant in the 35th Sikhs, Lieut.-Colonel Goldney, marked his promotion out of the regiment to the command of the 36th by the following complimentary order, dated Nowgong, November 9, 1894:—

"The Commanding Officer takes this opportunity of conveying to Major Haughton the great regret which he, the officers, native officers, and the rank-and-file feel at his having left the regiment. His removal to a higher position, for which he is so fitted, deprives the regiment of a thorough soldier, an efficient officer, and a good friend; and in bidding him farewell, Lieut.-Colonel Goldney feels sure that all ranks join him in wishing Major Haughton every success in the future."

At Bannu in December, 1894, commenced Major Haughton's experience of frontier service. Up to that time Ferozpur, Amritsar, and Lahore were the most westerly stations to which service in India had called him. He had not been three years on the frontier when war with the Afridis put his capabilities to the test. As all know, he came out of that ordeal with the highest credit and honour to himself. Five months at Bannu were followed by twenty months at Peshawar. In November, 1895, he was made a temporary Lieut.-Colonel under the new warrant. Just before Christmas, 1896, the 36th Sikhs moved from Peshawar to Kohat, and in 1897 were ordered to garrison the Samana forts. Mrs. Haughton accompanied her husband, and stayed with him at Fort Lockhart till May, 1897, when she went to England. She thus escaped the trials which, as I shall presently tell, awaited Mrs. Des Vœux. A little daughter, named Helen Katherine, was born to Colonel Haughton on September 2, 1897, at Oxford. This was the eve of the first attack on the Fort of Gulistan, which took place on September 3 and 4, an account of which I am about to give in the next chapter.

NATIVE OFFICERS OF THE 36TH SIKHS. TIRAH, 1897.

CHAPTER VI.

THE DEFENCE OF THE SAMANA FORTS.

> "'Mid dark ravines, by precipices vast,
> Did there and here your dreadful conflict sway."
> ARCHBISHOP TRENCH.

WE now approach that period of Lieut.-Colonel Haughton's life, in which his capacity as a soldier and as a man, already sternly tested in the various trials that befall mankind, was to be put to the crucial test of active service. We have seen him pass through the ordeal of the loss of wife, father, and brother, and throughout it bear himself like a noble and Christian man. We have seen him selected to fill, firstly, an honourable though honorary staff appointment at the Delhi Camp of exercise; secondly, a *sub. pro tem.* wing command in a regiment which wanted specially able handling; thirdly, a permanent wing command in a newly raised frontier regiment (35th Sikhs); and fourthly, the command, at an unusually early age, of the 36th Sikhs, the sister battalion of the 35th. We may look upon each of these appointments as a case of special "selection." They show how highly he was thought of by his superiors. Throughout his letters which communicate these successive appointments to his friends we find a tone of unassumed modesty, at times even of diffidence in himself, coupled with a plainly expressed determination to try and do his duty in each and all of them. That he did his duty his successive promotions are the plainest proof. His friend and brother officer Major Gunning Hunter mentions how, from 1884 onwards, he devoted himself steadily and keenly to the study of books connected with his profession. When nominated in the summer of 1885 for duty as Brigade-Major at the coming manœuvres, he prepared himself for the task before him by a careful study of the Orders issued for the camp and of the Standing Orders of the Army. When sent to a Sikh regiment we find him at once studying the history of the Sikhs and the Panjabi dialect. When sent to the frontier in 1894 he learnt and passed an examination in Pashtu. Though this is compulsory for all officers serving in Pathan or frontier regiments, it is probably not compulsory for officers in Sikh regiments. When Colonel Haughton received his first—and, unhappily, last experience of active service, he was one who knew the native soldier thoroughly, and had been long enough at Bannu, Peshawar, and Kohat to pick up that knowledge of camp life and campaigning on the north-west frontier which is essential for a man who would lead troops against Pathan tribesmen. The one thing that he had not done was to lead his men in actual fighting. When he did do that, he evinced a genius as a leader of men such as few, if any, have surpassed or even equalled.

War and fighting are the touchstones of the character of the nation and of the individual, as the South African War has so well shown. Military training and discipline, despite all that such writers as Ouida and Mr. Stead may allege, exercise good influence on the citizen. The Peace Conference of 1899 (despite a little sentimental humbug, especially among ecclesiastics) and the South African War which so promptly followed it, have drawn from the best of our writers, orators, and preachers a wonderful unanimity of testimony to the value of war as a training-ground for mankind. The greatest English poet (Tennyson) and one of the best English prose writers (Ruskin) of the nineteenth century avow, in strong outbursts of eloquent feeling, their belief in war, and not in peace, as one of the great purifying and ennobling agencies of the world.*

It matters not whether the war be waged with the sword, the tongue, or the pen, in the arena of the battlefield, or on the floor of the House, in the pulpit, on the platform, or in print: it is in the stress of the struggle that the fibre of characters is formed and put to the test, that reputations are made or lost. A tame life is the lot of a tame nature. To prove ourselves men we *must* fight, be our methods

* In "Maud," and in the lecture on 'War' in "The Crown of Wild Olive."

of fighting what they may. Those who prate of universal peace would rob the very salt of the world of its savour, and, in so doing (strange irony), themselves (a miserable minority) cast down the gauntlet to the rest of mankind. The peacemonger heeds little that "charity" which St. Paul preached.

Haughton prated not of peace, nor did he seek to take offence lightly. It is rare in his letters to find him adducing arguments in his own favour; but (in a letter to his father) in commenting on his one serious dispute during his service, he remarked that it had been in his favour that he had never previously had any disagreement with any officer, senior or junior. He was a man who took up a clear and firm, but not aggressive, attitude in all his relations with his fellow-men; and there is no doubt that this definite style of action is a very potent preventative of misunderstanding and consequent mischief. We see it in the minor relations of everyday life; we trace it in the great problems of international politics. A wavering parent produces a disobedient child. Diplomatic shilly-shallying may provoke a war which plain speech would have obviated. "Wobbling" is a fertile source of evil. Haughton was no "wobbler." He was straightforward, firm, and true to the core. That is his moral character in a nutshell. We have now to portray him also as a leader of men in battle.

The year 1897, which, as being that of the Diamond Jubilee of her Majesty the Queen, should, to satisfy every loyal Briton, have been a year of ideal prosperity and peace, was, unfortunately, in India, a year of trouble. Yet there can be no doubt that such seasons of trouble bring blessings in their train, and out of seeming evil comes good. Famine and plague in India were met by unflinching efforts on the part of the Government and officials of that dependency, while private charity in Great Britain and the Colonies contributed more than generously to the good work of relief. The same has been done in 1900, despite the millions contributed to the comfort of our soldiers in South Africa and their families at home. If a certain semi-educated section of the native middle-class in India paraded its disloyalty in the summer of 1897, that has been more than counterbalanced by the splendid loyalty exhibited by the princes and nobles of that country, both during the frontier warfare of that year and more recently during our war in South Africa and China. If war be indeed a thing to be avoided as far as possible, nevertheless there are moments when it is felt that war comes not inopportunely. That the discontent of the frontier tribesmen must have taken overt form, sooner or later, there is little doubt. Coming as war did in 1897, when no other serious ties fettered either the Government or the Army of India, and when the Amir Abdurrahman Khan was firmly seated on his throne and strong enough to hold his own on either of his frontiers, it found us not unprepared, and not actively engaged elsewhere. Egypt alone at that time was locking up a few thousand British troops. A year later the victory at Omdurman, the defeat of French designs at Fashoda, and the success of our arms in Uganda had established British rule unequivocally in the Soudan. We were then free for South Africa. Our war there has been as opportune as that on the north-west frontier in 1897. Be it due to our national good fortune, or to the able diplomacy of our statesmen, our hands have, during both wars, been free from serious ties elsewhere. On the heels of either war has trodden trouble in China, a trouble in which we have been well able to support our own interests.

What has become known as "the rising on the north-west frontier," in 1897, fell unexpectedly upon India. The Tirah campaign was the final episode in the warlike operations which resulted from that "rising." The story of it has already been told, more or less, by other writers. I propose to tell here merely the part which Lieut.-Colonel John Haughton and, more indirectly, his regiment the 36th Sikhs, took in that campaign.*

* The 36th, like the 35th Sikhs, were raised in the hot weather of 1887. The two were sister battalions. As has been recorded, John Haughton assisted in raising the 35th, and has left on record that when he joined that corps at Ferozepur in May, 1887, "there were only about one hundred men in the regiment," and that "by August and September the regiment had reached its full strength of 912 of all ranks." I learn from the Indian papers that the 36th was raised by Colonel "Jim" Cooke and Captain H. R. Holmes, with Lieutenant (now Brevet-Major) C. R. Johnstone as Adjutant. Captain Holmes was the biggest and most powerful man of his time in the Indian Army, and performed at least one gallant act in saving life. It is said that when recruiting for the 36th Sikhs in the Ludhiana District, he used to challenge all and any to wrestle (the Sikhs are great wrestlers and fine athletes), the conditions being that the competitors should,

I have, in the main, based my account on hitherto unpublished papers, but for certain details and descriptions I am indebted to the *Times of India.*

The year 1900 may be regarded as the centenary of the north-west frontier of India, in that in 1800 the Government of that dependency first became alive to the fact that it had a frontier vulnerable to an enemy from Europe. It was in that year that the apprehension of a rumoured Russo-French invasion of India made the Governor-General despatch Captain John Malcolm on his first embassy to the Court of the Shah of Persia. Again, 1900 may be regarded as the jubilee of the same frontier, for early in 1850 Sir Colin Campbell led our first frontier expedition against the Adam Khel Afridis. General Sir Henry (then Lieutenant) Norman was his Brigade-Major. The 60th Rifles took part in this foray, and pitted their rifles against the Pathan jezail. At that time, it is believed, no other infantry in India had rifled firearms. The Afridi early established his reputation as a dangerous enemy in the hills. Mr. (now Sir Richard) Temple, when secretary to the Panjab Government, writing in or about 1860, describes the Afridi thus: "As soldiers they are amongst the best on the frontier. They

if worsted, enlist. This novel method so stimulated the recruiting, that the regiment is said to have been fit to appear before the Commander-in-Chief at a camp of exercise at Meerut during the cold weather of 1887–88. In 1891 the regiment left Delhi for Manipur, 777 strong, every man being five feet eight inches, or over, and thirty-six inches round the chest. Captain Holmes, having done his duty in raising a regiment physically worthy of his own splendid physique, retired from the Army in 1892.

are good shots. Their tactics resemble those of the other tribes. They retreat before the foe as he advances, and press upon him as he retires." That gives their tactics in a nutshell. During and just after the Tirah expedition, the Press in India teemed with contributions from writers, obviously very inexperienced, who appeared to think that the Pathans had adopted new tactics. Not so at all. The Afridis taught us nothing that Sir Colin Campbell, Sir Neville Chamberlain, Sir Sydney Cotton, and Sir Harry Lumsden did not know forty years ago, and which many other frontier leaders have learned since. The Afridis were faithful to their old Fabian tactics, almost to a fault. One new feature was introduced into the fighting. Many of the Pathans were armed with long-range and rapid-firing breech-loaders, and used smokeless ammunition. (*Vide* Appendix A.)

When the Afridi and Orakzai * clans rose against the Government of India in August, 1897, Lieut.-Colonel Haughton with his regiment was holding the forts and fortified posts on the Samana range, which runs westward from Hangu, an important post situated about twenty-five miles west of Kohat. The Samana range has the Khanki valley on its north and the Miranzai valley on the south. The Government of India, except in the direction of the Khyber, which was left to its fate, had taken prompt

* The chief sections of the Orakzai are four—namely, Daulatzai, Ismailzai, Lashkarzai, and Hamsaya. The whole clan is also split into two factions—Sāmil and Gār.

military measures to meet and cope with the danger that threatened our frontier outposts from Peshawar to the Kurram valley. Major-General Yeatman-Biggs was placed in command at Hangu, having at his disposal a body of troops aggregating the strength of a weak division.

The main positions occupied by the 36th Sikhs on the crest of the Samana ridge were the two fortified posts known as Fort Lockhart (or Mastan) and Fort Cavagnari (or Gulistan), the former being about nine and the latter twelve miles west of Hangu. Both these forts, which had been erected soon after the Miranzai expedition under Sir William Lockhart in 1881, were rectangular in form, and had stone walls from twelve to fifteen feet in height. To each was attached a small hornwork, the walls of which were very much lower.*

In each fort flank defence was provided by loop-holed bastions at diagonally opposite corners. Fort Lockhart could hold about three hundred, Fort Gulistan about two hundred men. In addition to these, picquet posts, somewhat similarly protected, had been established at Saragarhi (about a mile and a half west of Fort Lockhart and a mile and three-quarters east of Gulistan), Dhar, and Sartop, and at the Crag and Sangar picquets. These were built

* "The so-called hornwork at Fort Gulistan is an enclosure about eighty yards long by thirty broad, having the fort on one side, and being surrounded by a wall of loose stones (in local parlance, a "sangar") on the other three sides. This wall had been temporarily improved in places by logs of firewood, and by flour bags and kerosine tins filled with earth to give a little head cover to the troops."—*Pioneer*.

to accommodate each a garrison of from twenty-five to fifty men in strength. We find, however, that Saragarhi, which was considered the most important of these minor forts, in that through it signalling communication was maintained between Forts Lockhart and Gulistan and along the Samana range, was held by twenty-one men only.

Sangar was held by forty-four rifles, and a reinforcement of a native officer and thirty-seven men was sent to Dhar by Colonel Haughton during the first attack of the Orakzais on the Samana. As they each subsequently had to stand a siege of thirty-two hours, it was well that they were properly manned. In addition to these posts, which were all held by the 36th Sikhs, there were four others held by the border military police and by tribal levies, viz. Lakka, Tsalai, Gogra, and Saifuldarra. As will be seen by a reference to the map, all these eleven forts, large and small, are situated on the crest of the Samana range, except Saifuldarra, which is close to the right bank of the Khanki river.

On August 25 information was received that a large force (or "lashkar," in local parlance) of Orakzais was assembling at Karappa, near the tri-junction of the Chagru, Sampagha, and Khanki valleys. (I may mention that the fighting strength of the Orakzais and of the Afridis is stated to be approximately twenty-five thousand men each.) This force was afterwards estimated at twelve thousand men. It was considered inadvisable by those in chief military and political authority to precipitate hostilities by attacking this "lashkar." The advantage of the initiative was thus lost, and one or two of the minor Samana posts suffered before help could be sent to them from Hangu. On August 27 this Orakzai force made a general attack on the posts all along the Samana ridge. The police posts at Lakka and Saifuldarra, at the east end, were captured and destroyed. Soon after daybreak the enemy appeared in force on the Samana Suk, about a mile west of Fort Gulistan, which was held by Major Des Vœux with a hundred and fifty rifles. When intelligence of this reached Lieut.-Colonel Haughton at Fort Lockhart, he started at once with two British officers and a hundred and thirty rifles to support Gulistan. In the mean time Major Des Vœux had reconnoitred towards Samana Suk, but, finding that the enemy mustered some thousands, retired. Lieut.-Colonel Haughton, on his arrival, seeing that he was so outnumbered that any operation in the open was out of the question, withdrew all the troops inside the fort of Gulistan. The Orakzais occupying high ground about half a mile west of the fort opened on it a fire, which its inmates found very trying. Mrs. Des Vœux and her children and a nurse named Teresa McGrath were among those inmates. To check the enemy's fire Lieut.-Colonel Haughton sent Lieutenants Munn and Blair with half a company to "Piquet Hill," some three to four hundred yards west of the fort. This party was shortly afterwards withdrawn, but not until Lieutenant Blair had been dangerously wounded, a Snider bullet piercing the lung. "An inch higher," writes the *Times of India* correspondent, "would have severed the main artery; two inches lower would have penetrated the heart." His recovery, which was complete, is remarkable; but that wound prevented his taking that prominent part in the later defence of Gulistan which would have doubtless won for him some mark of distinction. In the afternoon Colonel Haughton heard that the eastern end of the range was also being attacked. He at once sent back to Fort Lockhart half the detachment which he had brought with him in the morning. Later in the evening, when the Orakzais withdrew from before Gulistan, he once more reconnoitred as far as the Samana Suk, from which he could see the enemy occupying the Chagru Kotal. On the morning of the 28th he returned to Fort Lockhart, and learnt that the forts at Gogra and Tsalai had been destroyed by the enemy. The border police, or levies, appear to have made no attempt to defend any of these posts, but abandoned them with a timely discretion that secured their own lives.

The latest departure in frontier policy is an organization of frontier militia under British officers. It is a purely probationary policy, of which time alone can attest the value. The "border militia," or "levies," which have been in use on the frontier for the last half-century, appear to have always known the right moment to "save their own skins." The Panjab Government appears to have recognized this right to "save their own skins" as one of their privileges. Usually when we employ and pay troops, we expect them to do the duty for which they are employed and paid, viz. in this case to defend their posts and protect our subjects. We must presume that the abandonment of the Khyber Rifles to their fate in August, 1897, was simply an extension of this policy of leaving the border militia, or levies, to shift for themselves. As it involved, however, the closing of the Khyber Pass, and therefore of all traffic between Peshawar and Kabul, the loss of fifty thousand rounds of ammunition, and the withdrawal of Captain Barton from his post of command, it could not fail to attract further attention, with results that are now sufficiently well known and have been amply, albeit justly, criticized.

A suggestion has been made that the Sikhs, the hereditary foes of the Pathans, should be planted along the border in posts or small colonies, and that to them a free hand should be given to check Pathan raids. The suggestion appears to have attracted no official attention; but that does not argue its impracticability or worthlessness.

Although the Orakzai lashkars (both *Sāmil* and *Gār*, so called after the two factions of the clan) continued to swarm on and around the Samanạ range, no further active attack was made by them until September 3. They wasted their time and opportunities in petty acts of destruction or outrage, or in mere "sniping" by day and by night. At daybreak on September 3 intelligence reached Fort Lockhart that a large force of the enemy was advancing against Fort Gulistan from the Samana Suk. Haughton at once started for Gulistan with a small reinforcement, part of which he left to strengthen the Saragarhi post. He came under a heavy fire on his way, and, on reaching Gulistan, found the enemy had planted their standards and established themselves in force on the south and west of the fort, within from two hundred to four hundred yards of the walls. They had succeeded also in creeping up and setting fire to the thorn abattis, which was pegged down and weighted with stones, a few yards outside the hornwork. This fire had to be put out twice by a sortie of unarmed volunteers from the garrison under a heavy fire at very close range. The task was one of very great danger, but it was done, and gallantly done, under cover of the fire from the walls. Sunder Singh and Harma (or Harnam) Singh were the two sepoys who specially distinguished themselves in putting out the fire. This is only one of the many gallant acts performed by the 36th Sikhs during the frontier rising of 1897–98. Indeed, that very evening, after darkness fell, a second deed of daring was done. The growing severity of the enemy's fire argued increasing numbers, but in the dark nothing could be seen. A sudden rush was apprehended. In view of this contingency a great pile of wood had been prepared beforehand about a hundred yards outside the hornwork. It was decided to light it. Two sepoys, Wariam Singh and Gulab Singh, volunteered for this difficult and dangerous bit of work. Leaping over the wall, and running almost into the midst of the enemy, they accomplished it successfully, and got back without being hit.* The Orakzais had by this time, under cover of the dark, gathered in on all sides of the fort, and kept up a heavy fire, accompanied by shouts and yells and beating of tomtoms, until midnight. This fiendish noise may have been intended to cloak some endeavour to crawl up to and undermine the walls, as at Charikar in November, 1841. If so, the bonfire and the alertness of the garrison defeated any such intent. When day (September 4) broke, they had withdrawn beyond effective rifle range. Later on they disappeared altogether. Colonel Haughton then returned with his detachment to Fort Lockhart. The Orakzais, seeing this, promptly returned to the attack, and throughout the night of September 4 kept up a heavy fire on the fort of Gulistan. Little damage, however, was done, and the next day they again withdrew. From information received, it transpired that they were discouraged by their want of success, and their jirgahs decided that, unless the Afridis supported them, they would not renew their attacks. Simultaneously almost,

* Both these gallant men took part in a sortie, of which I shall speak later, on September 13, and both were then very severely wounded. Wariam Singh died of his wounds.

the Afridi jirgahs had met at Bagh on September 3, and decided to send a strong force to co-operate with the Orakzais in their attack on the Samana forts. Meantime General Yeatman-Biggs, having assembled at Hangu a force of the three arms aggregating about two thousand five hundred men, started on September 7 to carry supplies to the Samana forts, which by this time were on half rations, and to resist the attack by the combined Orakzai and Afridi lashkars which was reported to be imminent. He reached Fort Lockhart on the 8th, and camped there, sending his sappers and miners to repair and strengthen the Gulistan defences. On the 9th a reconnaissance was made to the Samana Suk, and it was ascertained that a strong force of Orakzais and Afridis had assembled near Khangarbur, at the junction of the Sampagha and Khanki valleys. Twenty-nine standards were counted. On the 10th further contingents of Afridis arrived. The combined Orakzai and Afridi lashkars were now estimated at from twenty to twenty-five thousand men. On the evening of the 10th the sappers and miners completed their work on the Gulistan defences and rejoined the main camp at Fort Lockhart. By the morning of the 11th the concentration of the Orakzai-Afridi army was completed; and information reached General Yeatman-Biggs that a body, some thousands strong, was moving eastwards down the Khanki valley. Apprehending that an attack was intended on the Kohat-Hangu road, he also marched his force eastward along the crest of the Samana. After fighting a rear-guard action towards evening and checking the enemy's movement eastwards, General Yeatman-Biggs was obliged, owing to want of water, to make for Hangu, where his force arrived late at night, and necessarily somewhat exhausted after a hard day's work. This move, unavoidable as it was, left the Orakzais and Afridis, who doubled back on their tracks, free to turn the whole strength of their attack on the Samana forts. The distribution of the 36th Sikhs was at this time, approximately, as follows:—*

At Fort Lockhart, 168 of all native ranks under Lieut.-Colonel Haughton and Lieutenant Munn (adjutant). At Gulistan (Fort Cavagnari), 175 native ranks under Major Des Vœux, with 2nd Lieutenant H. R. E. Pratt, and Surgeon-Captain C. B. Prall as medical officer. Lieutenant A. K. Blair was lying dangerously wounded in the hospital. As already mentioned, Mrs. Des Vœux, her children, and their nurse, Teresa McGrath, were also in the fort.

Saragarhi	...	21 Rifles
Dhar ...	...	37 Rifles under a native officer
Sangar	...	44 Rifles „ „ „
Sartop	...	21 Rifles

The Sangar post was attacked on the night of the 11th, and, again, for twenty-four hours from

* Three companies of the regiment were, it seems, detached in the Kurram valley.

13th to 14th, but the strength of its position enabled the garrison to repel all attacks.

When day broke on the 12th, the Orakzai-Afridi "lashkar" was seen to be in force near Gogra on the east, at the Samana Suk on the west, and round the Saragarhi post, thus severing Gulistan from Fort Lockhart. (Their total number has been variously estimated at from twelve to twenty thousand.) It was, therefore, no longer possible for Colonel Haughton to carry aid to Saragarhi or Gulistan, as he had done twice before. The enemy turned the brunt of their attack on the little post of Saragarhi. Thousands swarmed round it; other thousands invaded Gulistan; while a third body of the enemy cut off communication with Fort Lockhart. It was impossible for either Haughton or Des Vœux to venture into the open with any part of their small garrisons in order to aid the little party in Saragarhi. At an early stage of the attack the Pathans tried to rush the post, but were repulsed with loss. They then took shelter behind the rocks, and behind folds and dips of the ground, and so, working their way under cover close up to the walls, maintained an incessant fire on the garrison. When the rush, just mentioned, was repulsed, two Pathans remained behind, crouched in the dead angle, where no fire could touch them, and set to work to dig down the walls. This is an old and familiar trick in Pathan siege tactics. The garrison inside appeared to be quite unaware that these two men were at work undermining the wall. Major Des Vœux, who saw them clearly from Gulistan, endeavoured to warn the garrison by signal, but was seemingly not successful. Colonel Haughton, though Fort Lockhart was not actually attacked, could do little more than caution Saragarhi by signal not to waste the ammunition, of which they had four hundred rounds per man. About midday he sent Lieutenant Munn with a small party of the Royal Irish Regiment (men who had been left sick in the hospital by General Yeatman-Biggs), armed with Lee-Metford rifles, to a point a short distance from Fort Lockhart to try and create a diversion by long-range volleys. This had no effect. While the two men in the dead angle were steadily undermining the wall, the bulk of the assailants kept the attention of the garrison fully occupied. Such an incessant fire from a range of a few yards was kept up on the parapet that the defenders scarce dare show themselves. Under cover of this fire repeated attempts were made to set fire to and force the wooden doorway.*

* Some say the door was of wood only, others of wood studded with iron. When the news of the gallant defence and fall of Saragarhi post reached India, and when it became known that a wooden door and want of adequate flank defence had been the weak points that caused its fall, there was, and rightly, a strong feeling of indignation against the engineering negligence or incompetence that was responsible for the loss of the post and its gallant defenders. The door of the tower that defends the railway station at Chaman was found in the same state in 1897. Arrangements were then made to have that rectified. The selection of good sites for defensible posts on the north-west frontier of India is a task of great difficulty. To get a spot which is not commanded within rifle range, and which contains within it, or close under its walls, a good water-supply, is no easy matter. For careless construction there is no excuse. The men who put up wooden doorways ought to be left to defend them.

About three in the afternoon the signaller notified that ammunition was running short. Haughton then determined to make a final effort to help them. Leaving seventy or eighty men of his regiment behind under the command of Lieutenant Lillie, Royal Irish Regiment (left behind sick), and Second-Lieutenant Haslam (R.E.), he, with Lieutenant Munn and ninety rifles (Sikhs), advanced cautiously towards Saragarhi. When he had advanced a thousand yards or so, he saw the enemy swarm over the walls and in at the doorway, and knew that all was over. What had happened had been more clearly apparent to the garrison at Gulistan. Soon after three o'clock the wall at the dead angle was seen to fall in, leaving a large breach. Half an hour later the Pathans rushed the breach, at the same time forcing in the wooden door, which had been riddled and torn by rifle-fire. The Sikh sepoys fought to the bitter end. They knew that the traditions of Sikh and Pathan warranted neither the giving nor receiving of quarter. One sepoy secured the guard-room door inside, and used his rifle till he was burnt to death. His foes admit that he accounted for twenty of them before his end came. The capture of Saragarhi is said to have cost the Afridi-Orakzai Alliance from one hundred and eighty to two hundred lives. The Pathans, having destroyed the walls of the post and set fire to the buildings, left it.

Such are the bare facts of the defence and capture of Saragarhi. We tell and read them now

FORT LOCKHART. (FROM SARAGARHI, SHOWING THE INTERVENING COUNTRY, WHICH COLONEL HAUGHTON HAD TO TRAVERSE TO RELIEVE SARAGARHI.)

in cold blood. Let us try and picture to ourselves for one moment the actual scene on that 12th of September. Inside that little post twenty-one men fighting unflinchingly for their lives; outside thousands of Pathans working relentlessly to take the hated Sikh blood; at Gulistan, two miles off, the garrison, themselves invested and powerless to help, noting, with an intensity of feeling which we can hardly realize, that slow but steady demolition of the "dead angle" wall; and lastly, Colonel Haughton and his men at Fort Lockhart watching the scene with a terrible anxiety, and doing what was possible, in the face of intervening thousands of Pathans, to create a diversion in favour of the gallant few in Saragarhi. Nothing evidently was known at Fort Lockhart of the two men who were undermining the wall. When the imminence of danger seemed to justify the effort, however perilous, to aid the little garrison, Colonel Haughton pushed with his men to a distance of a thousand yards or more from Fort Lockhart. The risk of being cut off was great. The Pathans were threatening his right flank, and could only be checked by the fire from Fort Lockhart and by a flanking party detached to cover his right. How far he could have carried his emprise, had Saragarhi continued to hold out, or how it would have ended, we know not. He was the last man to leave a comrade unaided, if aid were possible. He was, however, destined to die, not in the relief of Saragarhi, but in covering the retreat at Shinkamar. We may sorrow for the sacrifice of these brave soldiers, but the Sikh nation, while it lasts, will never forget the glory of the defence. A monument on the Samana spur near Fort Lockhart, and a cairn on the site of the Saragarhi post, commemorate the gallantry of the defenders. A subscription, raised through the instrumentality of the *Pioneer*, produced a sum of about £2000, which has been utilized for the benefit of their wives and families.

We must now turn our attention to Fort Gulistan. In the forenoon, the enemy advancing from Samana Suk occupied Picquet Hill and other commanding points as they had done before. Major Des Vœux, seeing this, promptly manned the defences. The troops, once posted, remained at their posts without relief or rest for more than fifty hours. There was scarce time even to partake of food, so pressing and incessant was the enemy's attack. Major Des Vœux had taken the precaution to store inside the fort all the water he could; but that all did not suffice for the wants of the garrison;* especially when some forty wounded men had wounds to be dressed and thirst to be assuaged. At about 4 p.m. on September 12, when Saragarhi had fallen, the attack on Gulistan began in earnest. The construction of that fort had its weak points

* It was the same story at Charikar in 1841; at Dhulipgarh, held for Reynell Taylor by Fateh Khan Tiwana in 1848; and, in a way, at Chitral in 1895—the same story of which any frontier officer will have had some experience. No fort is safe unless it contains its own water-supply; and yet posts are again and again established, the water-supply of which is outside the fort, and often not even under cover of the fire of the garrison.

THE RUINS OF SARAGARHI.

(From photographs by Lieut.-Colonel John Haughton.)

like that of Saragarhi. The special weak points were the angles of each bastion. Major Des Vœux, forewarned, took the precaution of building a breast-work of ration bags right across the interior of the vulnerable angles, of posting a sentry there to listen for the sounds of mining, and of telling off a special party of ten men for defence, in case the enemy should penetrate the outer wall. Throughout the night of the 12th the Pathans kept up a steady fire on the fort; and when the 13th of September dawned, it was seen that they had crept up within twenty yards of the walls, and, taking advantage of every bank and fold of the ground, built up shelters for themselves of stones and rocks (Indicé, "sangar"), and planted their standards on this line of sangars. Major Des Vœux decided that the most effective blow could be dealt by a sudden sortie. A standard planted opposite to and twenty yards from the north-west angle of the hornwork was fixed on as the point for attack. Havildar Kala Singh with his section, seventeen men in all, volunteered for the work. It was then about eight o'clock. A heavy fire was opened from the fort's hornwork on the Pathan sangars, while Kala Singh and his men, slipping out of the position on the south side, crept along that face to the south-west corner, and then with fixed bayonets charged the sangar. The Pathan fire, however, checked them, and they were fain to throw themselves on their faces. Instantly, without orders, Havildar Sunder Sing and eleven other men leapt over the walls to their support, and, carrying the first party with them, charged the sangar, drove out the Pathans, captured three standards, and amid the ringing cheers of their comrades rescaled the hornwork walls. It was seen at once, however, that two men were missing. Instantly three sepoys were over the wall again, and, before the Pathans could recover from their surprise and alarm, had brought in the missing men, both gravely wounded. Thirteen of the twenty-nine men were more or less severely wounded; three, as it proved, mortally. The effect produced well repaid the loss. It put heart into the defenders and cowed the assailants. The garrison stood to their posts steadily and manfully, and every wounded man fit to stand and shoot returned to duty as soon as his wound had been dressed. Some did not even report their wounds till the relieving force arrived. The enemy kept up a close investment and heavy fire, but dared not make an assault. Just before dark field-guns were seen to be firing in the Miranzai valley from the direction of Doaba, and a message arrived from General Yeatman-Biggs * that he and his force would relieve them next day. The position remained the same throughout the night. Want of food, water, and rest were

* On receipt of intelligence that Gulistan was hard pressed, General Yeatman-Biggs at once sent off a signalling party of the 3rd Bengal Cavalry towards Doaba, to inform Gulistan that relief would reach them on the 14th; also four guns, with five squadrons as escort, along the Shināwari road, with orders to make a diversion by opening fire from the Miranzai valley below, on the heights near Gulistan. This fire not only encouraged the garrison, but persuaded the Pathans that General Yeatman-Biggs's advance and relief would be by Doaba. His move *viâ* Sangar and Fort Lockhart thus took them by surprise.

FORT GULISTAN, SHOWING SORTIE GATE THROUGH WHICH HAVILDAR KALA SINGH LED HIS SORTIE.

GULISTAN, OR FORT CAVAGNARI.

beginning to tell on the garrison, but no one dreamt of losing heart. Major Des Vœux sent off a letter to assure General Yeatman-Biggs that his garrison was able to hold out, but the message miscarried. Daybreak on the 14th showed a force of Orakzais and Afridis, estimated at ten or twelve thousand, investing the fort, crowning Picquet Hill and the Saragarhi heights, and swarming on Samana Suk. An hour or two later the sound of field-guns was again heard, and by 9 or 10 a.m. shells were seen bursting over the heights near Saragarhi. The enemy located there promptly retreated down the northern slopes of the Samana to the Khanki valley. As the relieving force drew nearer and reached the Saragarhi heights, the Pathans drew off from Gulistan towards the Samana Suk. Then it was that Major Des Vœux and his men let them have the full effect of their rifle-fire from the fort. Many were seen to fall as they disappeared westward beyond the Samana Suk. The relieving force reached Gulistan at 1 p.m. It is estimated (officially) that the Orakzais and Afridis lost four hundred killed and six hundred wounded in their unsuccessful attack on the Samana forts. Of the 36th Sikhs, twenty-one men were killed at Saragarhi; while at Gulistan two were killed and thirty-nine wounded, of whom eight dangerously. One officer (Lieutenant Blair) was dangerously wounded. Havildar Kala Sing, who led the sortie, was one of those who succumbed to his wounds. Major Des Vœux's wife and children escaped unhurt. Teresa

McGrath, their nurse, showed great courage and fortitude, attending to the wounded, and helping in any way she could without thought for herself. Her Majesty afterwards conferred upon her the Royal Red Cross. I will conclude by quoting the words of an eye-witness, one of the relieving force—

"Fort Gulistan was safe, and with lightened heart some of us pushed on. By 2 p.m. we were within its walls. Blackened with gunpowder, worn out with forty-eight hours * of continuous toil and stress, many bandaged and blood-stained, the garrison still preserved a brave front. Drawn up at the gateway were the survivors of the sortie, with the three standards they had captured. Major Des Vœux, who had his anxieties doubly intensified by the presence of his family, had been the life and soul of the defence, guarding against every danger, and showing a fine example of cheerfulness and steadfastness to all. Lieutenant Pratt, an officer of a year's standing, had ably seconded him, and Surgeon-Captain Prall had untiringly tended the wounded under heavy fire, helped by Miss Teresa McGrath, Mrs. Des Vœux's maid, who amid the flying bullets could be seen here bathing a wounded sepoy's head and there tying up another's arm till the doctor could come. Last, but not least, every sepoy of this gallant band did his duty, and at times almost more than his duty, in a way worthy of the proud name of Sikh."

Regarding the movement of the relief force, it

* They were under arms from 9 a.m. on the 12th to 1 p.m. on the 14th; in all, fifty-two hours. "One of the grandest feats of arms in the South African War was the defence of Jammersberg Drift, where seventeen hundred men of the Colonial Division kept eight thousand of the enemy at bay for seventeen days, every man staying at his post in the trenches, without warm meals for days on end and up to their knees in water."—General Brabant's speech at Cape Town, July, 1900.

suffices to say that General Yeatman-Biggs, with eighteen hundred infantry and four guns, left Hangu at midnight on September 13, and by eight next morning had driven the Pathans off the Gogra Spur, and relieved the Dhar and Sangar posts, which were only less hard pressed than Gulistan. The garrison of Sangar had also made a sortie and captured a standard, which they proudly displayed to the column of relief as it passed. As the advance guard of General Yeatman-Biggs's force approached, the garrison of Sangar and that of Fort Lockhart, under Colonel Haughton, sallied forth and opened fire on the enemy retreating to the Khanki valley. By 10 a.m. Fort Lockhart was reached. Colonel Haughton and his men then joined in the movement to relieve Gulistan. The heights of Saragarhi were still held by some thousands of the enemy, and it was not till they were driven off and those heights gained by our own troops that it was known for certain that Gulistan was still safe. The 2nd Panjab Infantry and Colonel Haughton's Sikhs hurried on to attack the thousands of Pathans who still swarmed round Gulistan. They, however, gave our troops no chance of closing with them. General Yeatman-Biggs and his force camped that night near Fort Lockhart, the 2nd Panjab Infantry and two guns being left to protect Gulistan. On the 15th and following days fresh-water tanks were dug on the Samana, and the roads and telegraph lines repaired. Hostilities, however, were not destined to be resumed there. On the 16th a reconnaissance was made beyond the Samana Suk to within a mile of Karappa in the Khanki valley. Everything seen and heard indicated that the Afridi-Orakzai "lashkar" had, for the time being, dispersed.

The following is Colonel Haughton's own account written to his wife. It is full of interest.

"Fort Lockhart, September 13, 1897.

"Yesterday was a terrible day, for I saw twenty-one of our gallant men slaughtered at Saragarhi, and was unable to do anything to prevent it. On the 11th great numbers of the enemy were seen going off in the direction of Hangu; and the General, being fearful for the safety of the small camp there, went off with his force in the evening to save Hangu. His force went down by the Saifuldarra road, or, rather, along the hills that way. They were engaged with the enemy from 10 p.m. to 4.30 the next morning; we could see the fight going on, but could do nothing. I hear we had only about two or three killed, and the enemy had fifteen or sixteen. The situation at 9 a.m. on the 12th was as follows. The enemy were in great force on the next hill beyond Sangar (where there used to be a police post called Gogra). Another force, numbering many thousands, appeared on the hills at Saragarhi (that is, between this and Gulistan), and there were a lot more between here and Saragarhi, below the crests of the hills. They simply swarmed on the hills near Saragarhi, which post they surrounded at a short distance, and kept firing at. At twelve o'clock Saragarhi signalled that they had one sepoy killed and one Naik wounded, and three rifles broken by the enemy's bullets. Mr. Munn took out twelve men of the Royal Irish (who had been left here sick and as signallers), and tried to fire long-range volleys at the enemy, who were visible from here, though sheltered by rocks from the

Saragarhi fort. We saw the enemy make at least two assaults on the post, but they were driven back. At three o'clock I came to the determination, at all costs, to try and make some diversion ; so, as soon as possible afterwards, Mr. Munn and I with ninety-eight rifles went out, leaving seventy-three men to defend Fort Lockhart. We had to go very cautiously, as our spies reported a strong force of Afridis below the hills, to the right of the road between this and Saragarhi. We had only gone about three-quarters of a mile when we saw Saragarhi taken by the enemy. Of course it is difficult to say what occurred, but from our own observations and from reports, it seems that the enemy managed to break down the door of the post (a wooden one—a fearful mistake), and then our poor men ran down from the parapet to defend the doorway.

"September 15, 1897.

"I was interrupted and had to stop. I am not sure whether the above is quite correct—that is, whether the door was broken in or not ; but Major Des Vœux, who was surrounded at Gulistan, saw the Pathans at Saragarhi making a hole in a dead angle in the wall. They got in there, and our men ran down to defend the hole, and the enemy immediately swarmed over the walls. The end was not long, though it is said that one poor fellow defended himself in the guard-room and shot twenty of the enemy inside the post. The brutes then set the place on fire. Meanwhile Gulistan was being attacked, and, after the fall of Saragarhi, its captors went off to help the Pathans at Gulistan, leaving some thousands at Saragarhi, to prevent succour going to Gulistan. They attacked all that day and night. The next morning things were very critical, and Major Des Vœux gave leave to a Havildar and sixteen men, who had volunteered, to make a sortie. These gallant fellows went out of the hornwork gate, ran along outside the hornwork and attacked a party of the enemy who had planted their standards under a crest of the hill, only about twenty yards beyond the end of the hornwork. They were having a bad time of it, when another Havildar and eleven men got over the end of the hornwork and went to their aid. This turned the scale, and the gallant little party drove the enemy back at this point and took three of their standards. Out of the seventeen who first went out, eleven were wounded, as well as several of the second party. When they got back they found that a wounded man was left behind, and they again went out and brought him in. Nothing could have been more gallant. I regret to say that of the two Havildars one is already dead, and the other, I fear, cannot live. That sortie had a wonderfully depressing effect on the enemy, and a splendid effect on all our men. No assistance could come to Gulistan for another twenty-four hours, and of course it was a fearfully anxious time for us at Fort Lockhart. It is impossible to describe what an anxious time it must have been for Major Des Vœux.

"The General sent a field-battery on the evening of the 13th to the foot of the hill. Of course it could not get up, but it sent some shells pretty near the enemy, which, though they may not have done much harm, had a good moral effect. During all that night I listened anxiously, and was very thankful whenever I heard a shot from Gulistan. We, that night and the night before, had a few shots fired into us, but it was only what is commonly called 'sniping.'

"September 16, 1897.

"However, it had this bad effect: I had intended starting off at 3.30 a.m., with every man I could spare, to go out and meet the General's force, and fire into the rear of the enemy, whom he would be attacking in front. Taking the sniping parties into consideration, and that the enemy were in thousands at Saragarhi, and possibly nearer, which meant that they would at any rate be nearer Fort Lockhart than I should be when I went out to meet the general, I gave up the plan for the time. However, at about seven o'clock Mr. Munn, with thirty of our men and about a dozen of the Royal Irish, went out and got down to a bit of a hill below Sangar, where we were able to get some good though long-range volleys into the enemy as they retired before the General. They did not make much resistance directly they heard the guns. I cannot say what damage our volleys did to them, as they were so scattered about over the hill-side, but we could see our bullets going all in among them and knocking up the dust. About those same guns (four of Captain Parker's Mountain Battery), they had gone up the Kurram with Colonel Richardson's column, but when the General found they were more wanted here than there, they marched back seventy-two miles in seventy hours; then, after a day's rest, they came on with the General from Hangu to Gulistan. Well, to continue: as soon as the enemy had fled from their position beyond Sangar, the General said he must push on hard to Gulistan. So we with our few men raced back to Fort Lockhart, got all the men we had left there out, and, without asking permission, stuck ourselves at the head of the General's force. The enemy were pretty strong at Sangar, and we thought they would fight; so, unfortunately as it turned out, the General determined to shell the place before the infantry advanced. Consequently the enemy disappeared behind the ridge. We thought they would wait there till the advance of our own infantry prevented the guns firing, and would then jump up and give us a busy time. However, when the 36th and 2nd Panjab Infantry advanced over the hill there was not a man left. Poor Saragarhi was absolutely a heap of stones, but amongst the ruins we could distinguish the remains of our poor fellows, hacked to pieces by these fiends.

Then, when we got beyond the Saragarhi heights and could see Gulistan, we saw the enemy as thick as peas round it ; but they bolted like French partridges as soon as we showed our noses a mile and a half off, and, unfortunately, it was a long time before the guns could get up. When they did get up there were very few of the enemy left within range ; and though the guns opened a pretty accurate fire, I don't fancy the enemy could have suffered much. We found our people at Gulistan very cheery. The General is awfully pleased with all our men ; I think they have just done splendidly. Mrs. Des Vœux is wonderful ; she had had pretty high fever, but the morning of our arrival her temperature was normal. She was very cheerful, and looked wonderfully well. Teresa has just been splendid,* nursing the wounded, etc.

"I am sorry to say, out of the garrison of 121 there were forty-one wounded (not counting those wounded before), many of them very severely. Several have since died, and I fear more will die. Dr. Prall worked like a horse, or like a whole team of horses. Major Des Vœux reports that Mr. Pratt did splendidly. I hope he and Major Des Vœux and Dr. Prall will be well rewarded."

* Extract from letter dated September 5, 1897—

"Fort Lockhart.

"Teresa has been simply splendid, looking after the children and baking bread by day and looking after Mr. Blair at night, besides superintending food for both patients. She has been as plucky and cheery as possible, and on more than one occasion ran down, under fire, from the fort to the hornwork to get things wanted."

THE SURVIVORS OF THE SORTIE PARTIES AT GULISTAN.
(*From photographs by Lieut.-Colonel John Haughton.*)

CHAPTER VII.

RAISING THE "PARDAH" OF TIRAH.

> "'Tis well in peril's darkest hour to find,
> Prompt for each turn of fate, some master-mind,
> Safe in success, in danger undismayed,
> Who . . .
> Rallies the broken ranks with skilful hand,
> And whilst one file remains, shall still command."
>
> "*Caubul*," *by* ZETA.

FROM the "sturm und drang" of the first half of September on the Samana, Colonel Haughton and his regiment passed to a month of comparative quiet, varied only by the preparation necessary for the expedition into Tirah. On October 17 Sir William Lockhart's "Orders" directed that "on October 21 a column under Colonel Chaytor, composed of the Northampton regiment, the 36th Sikhs, and No. 9 Mountain Battery Royal Artillery, should move from Samana to the Talai spur, to protect the right flank of the 3rd Brigade, moving in the Chagru valley." This order indicates the part played by the 36th Sikhs in the famous taking and retaking of the Dargai heights on October 18 and 20. When Dargai was being won from the tribesmen by Generals Westmacott and

Kempster on the 18th, it was necessary that the Samana forts should be secured from attack. On the 20th, when Kempster's Brigade, aided by the Gordon Highlanders and 3rd Sikhs, were stubbornly forcing their way to the Dargai heights, the 36th Sikhs were posted on the Samana Suk, their orders being to guard the right flank of the 3rd Brigade in its march down the Karappa defile. The Northampton regiment and No. 9 Mountain Battery were also there. Samana Suk is about on a level with and 2500 yards distant from the Dargai crest. The fire of No. 9 Mountain Battery was therefore brought into play with effect. We can imagine with what intense interest all on the Samana Suk must have watched the stern fight which Generals Yeatman-Biggs and Kempster were waging against the tenacious tenants of the Dargai heights. To Colonel Haughton and his men, burning as they must have been to avenge the butchery of Saragarhi, such inaction would be hard to bear. Duty, however, demanded it. In a letter dated "December 1, 1897, Camp Bagh," Colonel Haughton has recorded his opinion of the Dargai affair—

"What happened was this. The position at Dargai has to be approached by a narrow path; then, after the path, comes a bit of cliff which gives cover to rest in. The 2nd Gurkhas were the first to go at it, and four officers and a certain number of men got across, two officers and a lot of men being killed and wounded. When they got to the above-mentioned shelter they still had another bit to do. Some of the Dorsets—a section of sixteen men, I think—then started, and every one except the officer was knocked over; and there is no doubt that both they and the Gurkhas then considered attack on that line impossible. Then the Gordons were sent at it, and very sensibly an arrangement was made that, when they were ready, every gun (of the artillery) was to shell the ridge from which the enemy was doing the damage for three minutes, and that then the Gordons would make a rush. This was done, and the Dorsets and Gurkhas kept up a tremendous fire on the crest, whilst the Gordons made their rush. By the time the Gordons (together with the Gurkhas who had got across alive) commenced to tackle the second bit of path, the enemy were on the run, and had nearly disappeared by the time they got to the top. Had this plan been followed out at first it is possible the first troops might have done as the Gordons did. All praise to the Gordons, but I don't see why the others, especially the Gurkhas who lost more heavily than any one, should be disparaged."

On October 21 Colonel Chaytor's column, accompanied by General Sir William Lockhart and his Staff, started to descend the Talai spur towards the Khanki valley. The description of the march given by Captain Shadwell is so good that I cannot do better than quote it.

"The road was found to be fairly good as far as Karappa, and this was largely owing to the fact that working parties had greatly improved it for some way down; but up the Talai the path became most difficult till the Khanki valley was reached; it was little more than a goat-track going down a very steep mountain side through thick scrub and bushes. The company of sappers and miners had to be busily at work cutting it away and removing boulders in order to allow the transport animals, which were following, to get along without their loads being brushed off. The column was a very small one; all the baggage was on a reduced scale, and what little resistance there was on reaching the neighbourhood of Karappa, was quickly overcome by the troops of the main column, and did not in the least affect the progress of the Fort Lockhart column. Nevertheless the 36th Sikhs, under Lieut.-Colonel Haughton, who were on rear-guard duty, only managed to reach Talai, half-way, and that at 2.30 a.m. next morning (23rd). They did not reach Camp Karappa till 6.30 p.m. the next evening, having been actually thirty hours or more engaged in marching a distance of twelve miles, and downhill the whole time. But this delay on the road was also due to the inefficient transport. The Northampton regiment was supplied with indifferent mules and ponies, and the 36th Sikhs only had donkeys; so, what with loads slipping and animals falling and blocking the way, the pace of the rear-guard in the worst parts of the road seldom exceeded a few hundred yards an hour. The difficulty of moving in such a mountainous country where there are no roads is enormous, more particularly when one transport driver has to attend to three beasts. As these animals reach places where they must jump, slip, or scramble down from one rock to another, some accident is bound to happen before long to the loads, no matter how well they have been put on. Frequently it happens that there is no room to draw aside from the so-called track to readjust loads, then everything is stopped; and when there are about twenty thousand transport animals the number of these breakdowns is everlasting."

This is an admirable picture of the difficulties of marching in the often unexplored countries that border on our Indian frontiers. It recalls many of my own experiences in the Afghan War, on the Russo-Afghan Boundary Commission, in the Burmese War (1886–88), and with the column which explored and annexed in the winter of 1887–88 the Burmese Shan States (some 10,000 square miles) as far east as the Salween river. I may add one feature to the picture, viz. that the "three beasts" are as a rule chained together, a most dangerous union in difficult ground. The driver, whose intelligence is extremely small, often omits to unlink the chains when a bad place has to be negotiated. The result is that the leading mule is pulled violently on to its back, or the rear mule dragged forcibly forward on its face; or occasionally that the entire trio is carried over the edge of the path. The Persian muleteer and the Panthay in China and the Shan States never fasten their mules together. The mules are taught to follow a leader. It is remarkable that, up to the present, the Indian Transport mule has developed little or no aptitude for marching in droves. The Transport authorities fully grasp the value of training mules to accustom themselves to be driven and not led, and, wherever there is Transport, efforts are made to train the mules accordingly. In vain. Some always break away, throw their loads and scamper off across country. The Persian and Panthay mules eschew these frivolities.

During the week spent by the Tirah Field Force at Karappa or Khangarbur—a trying time, owing to the sniping tactics of the enemy—Colonel

Haughton's regiment took its share of picquet and foraging duties, but had only one man wounded. When Sir William Lockhart decided to recommence his advance on October 28, the 36th Sikhs were detailed with the Northamptons, under Colonel Chaytor, to seize a high hill on the right flank of and overlooking the route that had to be followed —a hill which the enemy had occupied daily during the halt at Karappa. There was, therefore, reason to expect, not only a very stiff climb, but also a hard fight, before it could be seized. However, as Colonel Haughton's own account will show, the enemy were caught napping. The Northampton regiment and 36th Sikhs held their post all day and joined the new camp at Gandaki in the evening.

On October 29 the Sampagha pass was carried. Severe resistance was expected. Westmacott's Brigade (the 4th), to which the 36th Sikhs belonged, moved in support of the 2nd or Gaselee's Brigade. During the attack Westmacott gradually pushed the 36th Sikhs, supported by the King's Own Scottish Borderers, into the front line. The 36th Sikhs, coming abreast of the Yorkshire regiment, helped to carry the crest of the enemy's third position, the point that was most stubbornly defended. Overhanging the crest and the pathway were precipitous cliffs held by the Afridis, who had got the range and were pouring in a galling fire. How the 36th Sikhs drove them out, let Colonel Haughton himself tell in his letter on October 30 from the Mastura valley. In it he briefly recounts the work of his regiment on October 28 and 29.

"Mastura valley, October 30, 1897.

"The papers will have told you that we have taken the Sampagha pass. They may not have told you that the enemy's final position above the pass was taken by the 36th Sikhs. But of that more anon. I forget the day I despatched my last, but I think when I did so we expected a move the next day, but did not move after all. On the night of the 27th we got orders that the next day we, supported by the Northamptons, were to capture a high hill overlooking camp, which had been occupied every day by the enemy. We were to start an hour before daybreak, so as to be ready to commence the attack as soon as it was light enough. This we did, and, rather fortunately for us, found the enemy had left it at night. It was a fearful pull up, in many places almost perpendicular, and had we been opposed we should have had a stiff job. When we got to the top the enemy commenced potting us from the opposite hill, distant about 800 yards, and higher ground than we were, but we soon got under cover and commenced to build sangars. As soon as we had built them we got orders for the 36th to go off to another hill. Just the first few yards the enemy potted freely, but their fire was kept down by the Northamptons, and we were soon out of their sight. We had a fearful climb down and a still more fearful climb up, but got to our place at last. After we had been there some time, much to our delight orders came that we were to come down to the new camp and the Northamptons occupy our place. We got to camp at 4.30, having had nothing but a bit of chocolate and a biscuit since 4.30 a.m.

"*October* 29.—We had a fearfully hard day but not much

fighting.* . . . General Westmacott called me up and told me to attack the position covered by fire from the King's Own Scottish Borderers and the guns. I got a couple of companies together and we made a rush to some rocks about fifty yards and then on another fifty yards. Just that first hundred yards the enemy poured in a pretty hot fire, but we had only one man killed † and three wounded, thanks to the splendid fire kept up by the King's Own Scottish Borderers. After that there was hardly a shot fired at us, but it was a fearful pull up, and we were all dead beat by the time we got to the top. Captain Searle and I were the only officers with the leading companies. I believe I was the first man of the Army to see into this valley. I don't mean to say that other troops hadn't fighting, and some of them a good deal more than we did—still the fact remains that we were the first in and over the Sampagha pass."

The Tirah Field Force camped that night in the Mastura valley and rested there the following. "Beautifully fertile, intersected by a spring-fed rivulet of pure water, not closely wooded, yet there are many beautiful groves dotted about, and the autumn tints remind one of England." So writes the *Times of India* correspondent on October 30, 1897. On the 31st the 4th Brigade (Westmacott) supported by the second and third (Gaselee and Kempster) left camp soon after daybreak—the cold was bitter—to force the Arhanga pass. No resistance worth speaking of was made, and before 11 a.m.

* This describes the final act in the capture of the Sampagha pass.

† The sepoy killed is said to have been the tallest man in the regiment, taller even than Colonel Haughton himself.

THE CAMP OF THE TIRAH FIELD FORCE AT MAIDAN.

the crest of the pass was occupied by our troops. Captain C. T. A. Searle of the 36th Sikhs was severely wounded. By eventide the main body of Sir William Lockhart's force was encamped in the Maidan valley of Tirah, that maiden vale which the Afridi boasted had never before, in the annals of his clan at least, seen an invader. Maidan * is about 6400 feet above the sea level. The cold there in winter is bitter. At the end of October, however, and early in November, though the nights are chill and frosty the days are charming. The rains and snows had not yet set in, which, later on, caused such hardship and trial to Sir William Lockhart's troops.

* He who would read a good description of that valley, will find it in Captain Shadwell's "Lockhart's Advance through Tirah." Colonel Hutchinson's "Tirah" gives plans of the Sampagha and Arhanga passes, and views of the Mastura valley. In Mr. Lionel James's "Frontier War, 1897," are photographs of the Sampagha and Arhanga passes, and the Maidan valley and camp.

CHAPTER VIII.

SARAN-SAR AND TSERI-KANDAO.

"And that same season of our genial use,
It was your very agony of strife;
While each of these our golden moments sees
With you the ebbing of some noble life."

ARCHBISHOP TRENCH.

THE names I have set at the head of this chapter are those of two passes leading from the camp in Maidan; the one east-north-east into the Zakha Khel country, the other east by south into the Waran valley tenanted by the Aka Khel. "Khel" is a section of a tribe. The chief sections of the Afridi are Adam, Zakha, Kambar, Aka, Malikdin, Sipah, and Kuki. "Saran-Sar" means "head of heads" or "peak of peaks." "Tseri-Kandao" means "Oak-tree Pass," the word "Kandao" signifying in precise terms the "top of the pass."

During the ten days that elapsed between the arrival of the force at Maidan and the Saran-Sar reconnaissance the tribesmen were anything but quiescent. They harassed our camp and troops whenever opportunity offered. On the evening of November 6, Captain E. L. Sullivan of the 36th Sikhs was shot through the wrist, and had to be

THIS PANORAMA IS A CONTINUATION, TO THE RIGHT, OF THAT SHOWN IN THE PRECEDING ILLUSTRATION, ENTITLED "THE CAMP AT MAIDAN."

invalided to India. Captain Sullivan had only rejoined his regiment from England that very day, and became the victim of a "sniper" before he had been five hours in camp. On the morning of the same day, Captain Plunkett of the Manchester regiment, who, with an escort of the 36th Sikhs, was escorting a convoy into camp, was attacked by some two hundred Afridis. The Sikhs drove them off. On another occasion,

> "a party of Afridis crept down the wooded slopes to the west of the 4th Brigade camp, and attempted to rush an outlying picquet of the 36th Sikhs, who were in one of the villages across the central nullah. This attempt was abortive, as unwittingly the tribesmen exposed themselves to a flank fire from a picquet of the 3rd Gurkhas, also posted across the nullah." *

These three cases are a few of many illustrative of the harrying tactics of the Afridis.

It is not my intention to dwell in detail on the operations carried out from Maidan prior to the Saran-Sar reconnaissance. I may be excused, however, for saying a few words about the mosque at Bagh. It is an historic spot, as being the place where the Afridi elders of all clans meet in council. It is here that the Mulla Sayad Akbar preached the *jehad* (religious war), and it was here that the resolution was taken to go to war with the British Government in India. The mosque itself is described as—

* *Times of India* correspondent, dated "Tirah Plateau, November 2, 1897."

"insignificant, a mere oblong hut lying at the junction of three rivulets, under the lee of a bare hill, and shaded by fifteen or twenty trees. It has two walled and two open sides. Its mud roof is supported by twenty-one wooden pillars, a few of which are crudely carved. On the west wall is a niche for a lamp, and a small altar or pulpit with three steps. Some Korans were found in it. The floor was beaten and strewn with some very soft grass, a grass which no one recognized, so which presumably is rare. The two walls had at some period been whitewashed and rudely decorated with some black pigment, but time had almost completely obliterated this. On the north side was a little dark retiring-room, with a carved door and lintel; it was practically empty. The entrance to the mosque was a rough hole in the side of the plinth-wall, which was the foundation of the whole structure. The trees which shaded the temple were walnut and Himalayan oak; it is curious to note that the mosque did not lie east and west, but several points out.* Its dimensions were eleven by eighteen paces. Such was the spot where the Afridi and Orakzai resolved to wage war against the British Government. The gunners and Gurkhas ringed the trees of the grove." †

The act of barbarity mentioned in the last sentence, like the desecration of the Mahdi's tomb and grave, cannot be too much deplored. No plea, not even that of political expediency, can be accepted to excuse it. We would ourselves admit no such plea on behalf of the Mohammedans who desecrated our graves and places of worship.

* In this Mohammedan places of worship appear to resemble Christian.

† *Times of India* correspondent, *ut supra.*

THE MOSQUE AT BAGH IN TIRAH. (THE AFRIDI HOUSE OF ASSEMBLY.)

The strong expressions of indignation which the treatment of the Mahdi's tomb and body in 1898 elicited were well deserved. This minor act of sacrilege away in the wilds of Tirah passed unnoticed, but it is none the less to be regretted. It is an act to which we look back with anything but pride or satisfaction.

The reconnaissance to the Saran-Sar pass was directed to be made on November 9, and entrusted to General Westmacott's Brigade. It was notified that Sir William Lockhart and his Staff would accompany the force, which consisted of the Dorset and Northampton Regiments, the 15th and 36th Sikhs, and No. 8 British and No. 5 Bombay Mountain Batteries. The Saran-Sar pass leads from Maidan into the Bara valley, and thence to Peshawar. It is, therefore, a route of high importance, and one that had to be surveyed. The distance from the camp to the foot of the hills was barely three miles, but the country was hummocky and intricate, and cut up by deep precipitous ravines. Near the base of the ascent to the pass stood a conical hill, from which the batteries came into action. Two spurs and a series of ridges, wooded in parts, lead to the foot of a steep cliff, round the base of which winds the pass over the summit of the Kotal, approximately 8650 feet above sea-level. At 11.30 a.m. the Northamptons, supported by the 36th Sikhs, had, after a very stiff climb and some little fighting, occupied the Kotal. The Bara valley was not visible from the summit, but Tirich Mir and the mountains of Kafiristan could be clearly seen. In one of the Zakha Khel houses a Sikh's quoit and blood-stained hair were found, a ghastly relic of Saragarhi. By 12.45, the survey officers having done their work, General Westmacott commenced his retirement, but a few minutes later received orders to stand fast, as Sir William Lockhart and his Staff wished to come up to the Kotal. This delay was fatal, as events proved. The retirement did not recommence till 2.10 p.m. With these facts by way of preface, I will now quote Colonel Haughton's own unofficial account—

"Camp, Tirah, Maidan, November 10.

"Yesterday was a fearfully hard day, and I fear I must add a disastrous day; but I am thankful to say the regiment, though it had about the hardest work of anybody, and eventually covered the retirement of the Northamptons, only lost three men wounded. . . . We paraded at 6.45 a.m. to reconnoitre a pass, said to lead to the Bazar valley. The Northamptons were to go direct for the pass, followed by sappers and miners, guns, and then the 15th Sikhs. The Dorsets were to be on the left and make a turning movement; we were to keep about five hundred yards to the right and to make a turning movement, and occupy a detached hill on the right.

"Of course that sounds simple enough, but the valley is cut up by deep ravines, with often precipitous banks sixty or a hundred feet high, and to get to a place one mile off, one has often to go two miles. Well, we managed our part, and there was very little opposition. We had a stiff climb to get to the top of our hill, but when we got there were told that the guns would come there, and that we had better tackle the big hill where the pass was. So down we had to come, and then go up the steep hill where there was no path and the hillside was fearful. The Northamptons had a path, steep enough and bad enough, but a racecourse compared with ours. Of course we were fired at a little, but the guns made good practice, and we and the Northamptons arrived at the top almost together without any casualties. The Dorsets on the left had a few.

"Well, the necessary reconnaissance had been made, and General Westmacott had given the order to commence the retirement, when a message came to say that we were to wait, as Udny, Lockhart, and the Headquarters Staff were coming up. . . . We were sent back to a ridge, with orders to retire in front of the Northamptons, and to move out to the same flank again, and retire the same way as we had come. We waited until some of the Northamptons had got back to us, and proceeded to carry out the order. When we had got about two-thirds of the way down, a Tommy came running back saying that reinforcements were needed, and that part of his regiment were cut to bits, and that the enemy in force were coming round their left. I had seen the Dorsets there, and as there had not been much firing, thought it was simply a Tommy who had lost his head, and moreover I thought, and still think, that the more men there were on the hill, the more difficult it would be to carry out the retirement. However, after that, Major Des Vœux came and said that Colonel Chaytor wanted me to take up a position to cover his retirement down the hill, so I did this. Later on more men straggled down, and said that the Northamptons couldn't move; so, though we were dead beat, I gave orders for the three companies with me to go up the hill again. I suppose it was the excitement, but if you had asked me an hour earlier, I should have said, or at any rate have thought, that I could not have got up the hill again to save my life. When we got to the ridge which we had previously occupied, I found that the Northamptons had extricated themselves from their difficulty more or less, but had about a dozen killed and wounded. I got them to retire through us, we holding the ridge, and another further back. We did this till I thought they had had plenty of time to retire to the bottom, then I got our own men down as quickly as I could. When we got to the foot of the second hill (the one we had first occupied in the morning) we found a party of Northamptons in a nullah to our right (*i.e.* our right whilst retiring). This may give you some idea.

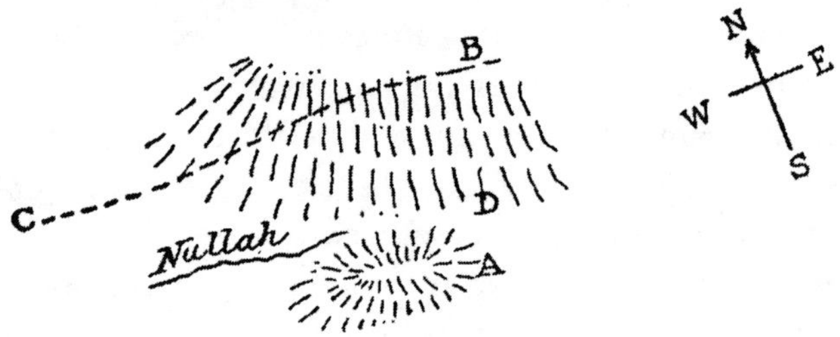

A is the hill we were first of all on. *B* is part of the big hill (called Saran-Sar). The dotted line is the road up, by which the Northamptons originally advanced. We originally advanced on top of *A* (and a jolly stiff climb, too), then descended northwards and ascended nearly straight up *B*. We retired round east of hill *A*, but when we got to the head of the nullah between the two hills, I saw a party of Northamptons in the nullah; they were being fired at by two or three men near *C*. I halted under cover near *D*, and sent Captain Custance and Mr. Munn on to *A* (from which the guns and troops had already retired). There were a few of the enemy firing from north and east and west, but we only had one man hit besides the two already mentioned, and we kept the enemy from advancing on the party of Northamptons in

General Westmacott.

BRIGADIER-GENERAL RICHARD WESTMACOTT AND STAFF.
(*From a photograph taken in Tirah by Lieut.-Colonel John Haughton.*)

FORT SARAGARHI IN RUINS, SHOWING THE MAIN ENTRANCE AND FORT LOCKHART IN THE DISTANCE.

the nullah, and we killed three of the enemy who had been firing from *C.* An officer and a few men came up from the nullah carrying a couple of wounded, and asked me for help to carry them. I sent him four men, and told him there were, I thought, some more of his men in the nullah. He sent back three men, who after about a quarter of an hour came back and said that they had all retired the other way. We had been detained about an hour at this place, and it was beginning to get dark, so I then retired as I had been told to do. We were fired at, of course, but got in about 7 p.m. That party lost themselves and were all killed. The Northamptons, I believe, lost two officers killed and one wounded, fourteen men killed and thirty-two wounded (some of whom have since died). The Dorsets had two officers wounded, one man killed and six wounded, 15th Sikhs one killed and four wounded, 36th Sikhs three wounded. So we must be thankful we got off so easily."

Had the retirement not been delayed, darkness would not have overtaken the troops before they reached camp, and the mishap of the Northamptons would not have occurred. It must, however, be noted that the 36th Sikhs, who covered the retirement of the Northamptons, suffered scarcely any loss. Several of the mishaps in the Tirah campaign were undoubtedly due to the inexperience and ignorance of frontier warfare of the officers and soldiers of our British regiments. It was to this that Sir George White afterwards so specially referred in his farewell order to the Indian Army. What a General *could* do in the retirement from Saran-Sar, General Westmacott did. I will just quote, from the *Times of India*, one or two remarks by eye-witnesses, which I find written a day or two after this affair—

(1) "The impression in camp is that if it had not been for the skilful handling of the retirement by General Westmacott, matters would have been far worse than they were." (2) "General Westmacott remained with the rear-guard to the end, and it is due to him that matters were not worse." (3) "In the retirement it was found that the men of G Company of the Northamptons were being wounded so fast that it exhausted the strength of the company. General Westmacott at once sent the 36th Sikhs to reinforce them, and this regiment, understanding its errand, made the second ascent magnificently, and the whole force was withdrawn to the base of the hill without further casualty."

It was then almost dusk. The enemy were relentless in their pursuit. Three miles of difficult country, intersected by ravines, had still to be traversed. Suffice it to say that the Northamptons stuck doggedly to their work, never abandoning a wounded man, while the 36th Sikhs covered their right flank. General Westmacott remained out till the last wounded man, as he thought, had passed on into camp, and then at 7.30 he came in himself with his rear-guard. Unfortunately, in the dark a small party of the Northamptons, consisting of an officer, a sergeant, and thirteen men, either took a wrong turning or were intercepted by the enemy. They were not missed at the time. Their dead bodies were found next day. They had fallen, evidently fighting to the last. Pathans rarely give quarter, though occasional cases can be mentioned

THE PULPIT, WITH LAMPSTAND AND COLLECTING-BOX COMBINED, OF MULLA SAYAD AKBAR. (*Taken in the camp, Maidan.*)

of prisoners being taken alive by them in action and spared. Captain Souter and others in 1842, and Lieutenants Fowler and Edwardes in 1895, are cases in point. A sergeant and private captured in the Bara valley in December, 1897, were also spared and returned alive.

The sad *finale* of the Saran-Sar reconnaissance caused no lull in the activity of the operations carried out from Maidan. On the 12th General Westmacott's Brigade was busy foraging northward, while on the 13th General Kempster's Brigade marched into the Waran valley, the 36th Sikhs occupying the Tseri-Kandao pass, in order to keep open the line of communication between the headquarter camp at Maidan and General Kempster in the Waran valley. Among the most interesting results of General Kempster's expedition were the destruction of the residence—a double-storied house with a small mosque—of the Mulla Sayad Akbar, and the discovery in it of some curious documentary evidence as to the causes of the frontier outbreak of 1897. One document found there was a manifesto from the notorious Hadda Mullah stating that "the Sultan (of Turkey) had completely crushed the infidels—referring to the Græco-Turkish War—in Europe, and had seized the approaches to India, and that the British being cut off from reinforcements, it was an auspicious moment for all Moslems to strike a blow for Islam." Other letters purporting to have come from General Ghulam Haidar, the Amir's Warden of the Marches, and other Afghan officials, were also found. These documents helped to throw some light on the motives which, coupled with fanaticism and resentment at or dread of encroachment, prompted the trans-frontier Pathans to rise, fortunately *seriatim* and not *en masse*, against us in 1897.

On November 16, General Kempster, having satisfactorily completed the task assigned to him in the Waran valley, commenced to return to the headquarter camp in Maidan. As usual, the Afridis (Aka and Zakha Khel) pressed hard on the retiring force, especially in the Tseri-Kandao defile, a pass five miles east of the main camp, leading from Maidan into the Waran and thence into the Mastura valleys. In this pass Colonel Haughton and the 36th Sikhs were posted to keep open communication and to cover the retirement. At daybreak on the 16th the 15th Sikhs left camp in Waran with orders to take over Tseri-Kandao from the 36th Sikhs. The Transport of General Kempster's Brigade reached the Maidan camp safely by 3 p.m. The 1st Battalion of the 2nd Gurkhas took the first turn of rear-guard duty, and were closely followed up by the Afridis to Tseri Kandao. There the 15th Sikhs relieved the 1/2nd Gurkhas; and were thus disposed: two companies under Captain O. W. Carey and Lieutenant T. L. R. Gordon were placed on the fir-clad slopes on the south of the pass; two companies on the bare rocky slopes north of it; further north still were two more companies commanded by Captain Lewarne and Lieutenant Vivian. These held the southern edge of the thick pine

Wood from which Afridis
made their attack.

TSERI-KANDAO PASS. SCENE OF HAUGHTON'S DEFENCE ON THE NIGHT OF THE 16TH OF NOVEMBER. GORDONS HALTED IN THE FOREGROUND.

woods that covered the summit of the long spur which ran down from Saran-Sar. Lieut.-Colonel Abbott himself with one company held the actual Kotal (*i.e.* east of the pass), while another company under Captain Rowcroft was placed on a commanding spot eight hundred yards in rear to cover the general retirement. All these companies were very weak ones. Such were the original dispositions, and for the time the enemy was held in check. As soon, however, as the 15th Sikhs endeavoured to retire from their position, the Afridis pressed them hard, especially Captain Lewarne's command. He repulsed their rush of swordsmen with volleys at very short range. His wounded, however, so encumbered him that he could not retire. From this point I will describe what occurred in Colonel Haughton's own words—

"Maidan, November 19.

"On the morning of the 16th our orders were that we would be relieved on the heights commanding the Kotal at 8 a.m. by the 15th Sikhs. We were then to march towards camp and take up positions on the heights commanding the road back to camp, with a view to the safety of the baggage, and we were finally to follow the rear-guard. It appears that the 2nd Gurkhas were rear-guard until they got past the 15th Sikhs. They seem to have been heavily attacked the other side of the Kotal, and had, amongst others, one British officer killed. They were much delayed, and did not get up to us until about 4 p.m.

"I had previously received two messages (one in writing) from General Kempster, commanding 3rd Brigade, to which we are temporarily attached, telling me to withdraw my regiment as soon as the Gurkhas got level with me. They (2nd Gurkhas) seemed a good deal exhausted, and were more or less encumbered with dead and wounded, so I allowed them to get on a good bit before I retired. General Kempster had passed me, and apparently approved of my dispositions. I was much surprised at the order to withdraw before the 15th Sikhs had come down, as it was contrary to my reading of my original orders, and I thought bad policy. However, the order to withdraw was quite plain. When we got back a few hundred yards, I heard that the 15th Sikhs were in difficulties and wanted help. General Kempster, thinking the whole business was over, had gone back to camp. His deputy-assistant adjutant-general suggested my going to a hill called Artillery Hill, but I pointed out that my doing so would not in any way help the 15th Sikhs to get away from the wooded hill on the left of the Kotal. He then said he would go and get a battery (which had gone on towards camp) to come back. When he had gone, I heard that the 15th Sikhs had so many killed and wounded that they could not retire without help (unless they abandoned their wounded). I immediately took the company that was with me and went off to the 15th Sikhs, and sent orders to the other companies to follow me as fast as possible. I should explain that companies were at intervals of some hundreds of yards, protecting the deep ravine on both sides down which the road runs. In fact the seven companies were spread over a very great extent of country. Had I sent a company to Artillery Hill they would have been isolated, would have done no good, as they could not see into several ravines by which the enemy would come down, and they would have had much greater difficulty in retiring than even the 15th Sikhs had. When I got up to the 15th Sikhs, I found Captain Custance with three companies had already got there. He and Colonel Abbott (15th Sikhs) had just been wounded when I arrived, and were sent back. The 15th Sikhs had been followed up through the wood, which was much too large to be held by their small numbers. They only had two very weak companies there. They had not got thirty yards from the edge of the wood before the enemy in considerable numbers appeared at the edge. I don't think there were more than sixty men of the 15th Sikhs. About a hundred or more of the enemy charged out of the wood and got up to about ten yards of the 15th. Very few of those hundred got back alive. When I arrived there were a great number of the enemy still firing from the edge of the wood, at about forty yards from our men who were nearest the wood. The enemy tried to get round our flank, but we nipped that in the bud. Gradually the fire slackened, and as it was beginning to get dark, and most of the wounded had been got down the hill, I made arrangements to retire, as, though we could not hope to get to camp that night, the position was untenable owing to the close proximity of the large wood, which was too big for us to hold. I think it is a proof that the enemy had more than they bargained for that we were not followed up, and hardly a shot fired whilst we were going down the hill. Halfway down I met Major Des Vœux with two companies. When we got to the bottom it was pitch dark. I reformed the two regiments—or rather those companies of them which were present—and we made in the direction of camp. We soon began to be fired on from three sides—not the side we had been fighting the enemy on. The worst fire came from some houses in the direction we were marching in, so I gave orders for both regiments to fix bayonets and go for the houses, which we did in good style. The enemy bolted, but Mr. Munn stuck one with his sword, and we must have wounded and killed several, although we only picked up one body in the morning. The road was fearful, intersected with precipitous ravines, and we (and the 15th) had a good number of wounded, and no stretchers or doolies to carry them, and were still several miles from camp; so I decided to stay the night where we were, as the houses and some banks gave a certain amount of protection. Major Des Vœux, with some fifty men, had got into some ruined buildings about one hundred yards further on, and the rest of us and the 15th got together at the buildings we had taken. Before we could make any sangars two or three of the enemy, who must have been hiding in our midst, jumped up and bolted, and in the pitch darkness, I fancy, got clean off, though probably some of them were wounded. It was just after this that Mr. Munn was shot through the hand when within a foot of me, and, while I was calling for the doctor, poor Captain Lewarne (15th Sikhs) was shot at my side. I believe he was shot through the heart, and his death was practically instantaneous. We managed to get up a few stone sangars, but it was impossible to do much, and the enemy, shooting from different directions, killed two or three of our men and wounded about the same number.

"The cold was intense. It was freezing hard. Our men had their cardigan jackets and capes, most of the officers nothing, and the half company of the Dorsets who were with us had nothing. I fortunately had my *poshtin*,* carried by a Rabia Khel from the Samana, but I did not find him till about midnight, and was very cold, being soaked in perspiration from the exertion of racing up the hill to the help of the 15th Sikhs. Mr. Turing had his *poshtin* carried by his orderly, but he did not get it till nearly morning, when he found the poor man, who had been shot dead when we first arrived at the place. We managed to

* Sheepskin coat.

find a sheltered spot for the wounded under the warm wall of the house, which had been burnt and was still smouldering, and we also found a clear spot on the warm embers where we got down half of the Dorsets at a time to get a little warmed up.

"I thanked God when there were signs of daylight. We sent out a reconnoitring party, and before daylight managed to get all the dead and wounded on to where Major Des Vœux was, as the intervening space was much exposed and would have been nasty to cross under fire with our wounded men. We got off, only a shot or two being fired at us, and met doolies and stretchers with a Brigade coming out about halfway to camp. Our (the 36th Sikhs) loss was two officers and seven men wounded, and six men killed, all of whom we brought back except one body. The 15th Sikhs lost one officer killed, one wounded, and about fourteen men killed and sixteen wounded. They brought in their wounded, but had to leave their dead behind. We had to improvise stretchers out of rifles and putties until we met the party coming out.

"Thank God things were no worse. There were many narrow escapes. Captain Custance had two bullets through his hat, besides being wounded in the thigh, Mr. Turing a bullet through his hat. Mr. Munn, besides being shot through the hand, had a sword-cut in the same hand (right) and a bullet through both legs of his trousers. Mr. Pratt lost his way, and with eight men of the Dorsets and two of ours, spent the night in a ruined house. He showed great presence of mind. Mr. Munn and Captain Custance are a great loss to the regiment. They are both splendid officers on service."

The effect of this successful all-night stand, made by Colonel Haughton on his own initiative and when left to his own resources, had a most admirable effect upon the troops serving in Tirah, and, indeed, on the entire Army in India. It, in short, established a precedent, showing how belated troops, when overtaken by the dark and hard pressed by Pathans, could best hope to hold their own. Moreover the enemy (Zakha, Aka, Kambar, and Sipah Khel) suffered severely—more severely, it is said, than in any other action in the campaign. That loss is fairly estimated at 300. Further, it showed the Pathans that there were amongst us officers and men who were quite equal to meeting and worsting them at their own game. The only previous similar stand with which my study of frontier warfare has acquainted me, was one made in October, 1841, by General Sale's force marching from Kabul to Jalalabad. When Nott was retiring from Kabul in October, 1842, his rear-guard and baggage was caught in the dark and sore pressed by Pathans; but a timely reinforcement sent out from camp extricated it, and brought in, so report says, every man and animal safe. The one incident which may be said to have marred the complete success of Colonel Haughton's clever plan of action, was due to the disobedience of orders and ignorant folly of a small detachment of the Dorset regiment, which Major Des Vœux had posted some way down the pass, when he himself was advancing to support Colonel Haughton and the 15th Sikhs. This party, consisting of two young attached officers and eleven men, are supposed, after a time, to have left their post and endeavoured to return to camp. They were all found dead in a nullah in the morning. Had they, like Mr. Pratt and his little party, remained where they were, they would have been safe.

When the news of this deed of arms reached India, it was greeted on all hands with the warmest expressions of approval. It was a bright spot—a deed to be justly proud of—amid a succession of incidents in our frontier fighting, from July, 1897, onwards, which had caused disappointment and, in one or two cases, more than disappointment. The officer in command had shown not only courage but presence of mind, endurance, and resource. Moreover, he had acted on his own initiative and responsibility. As I write these words I seem to see, looming before me, the word "STUPID," the epithet applied to the officers of our Army, after the Koornspruit affair, by a correspondent of the *Times*, endorsed in that journal by several "leaders," and solemnly discussed by a posse of prominent letter-writers. A voice from the Athenæum Club, using the same journal as mouthpiece, cried out upon "the humiliation" the country had experienced. If there be indeed "humiliation," surely it lies in the pessimism and defective knowledge that inspire such comment, and in the sensationalism that blinds a vast section of the Press and the Public to the dictates of truth and good feeling. "There is no new thing under the sun." A hundred and forty years ago Dr. Johnson

(*Idler* of November 11, 1758) sketched for us a prototype of the "latter-day journalist." *

* A special correspondent of the *Morning Post* commences a letter, dated Pretoria, June 28, 1900, with these words: "One realizes that our army was planned for almost any purpose but that of war," etc. This is one sample of the style and tone affected by the war correspondent of to-day. Such, in his self-confident opinion, is the British Army—the Army that in the last three years has upheld the interests of the Empire on the North-West Frontier of India and on the Gold Coast, in the Soudan and Uganda, in South Africa and China, and which is maintaining at this moment close on 300,000 men on active service at an average distance of 5000 miles from their base. This, too, is the Army which, in conjunction with our Navy, sets bounds to foreign hostility.

The fatuity of such criticism as I have quoted defies comment. Smartness, tempered by ignorance, is the characteristic of a number of the war correspondents evolved by the South African War. The young journalistic idea, like every other "young idea," wants forming. One of the duties which the twentieth century would appear to impose on the National Press, is the foundation of an University for the proper education of its journalists. The Church, the Law, and Medicine demand a degree or diploma. The Army, Navy, and Civil Services, Engineering, Science and Art, each exact the test of adequate training and examination. Journalism has no claim to exemption. Even heaven-born genius may gain by guidance.

We soldiers—often by hard and grievous experience—know, better than the journalist who writes *en amateur*, the weak points of our Army organization and administration; and we in India certainly know the faults, foibles, and failings of the Military Department. Despite this knowledge, we hold the opinion that the responsible persons are men who, according to their lights and subject to the over- or under-weight of human nature's handicap, try to do their duty.

The Army welcomes the advocacy and appreciates the criticism of the Press, when given temperately, in good taste, and with sound knowledge and judgment. When, as has happened so often in the last twelve months, these qualities are conspicuous by their absence, we can only regret the power the Press possesses and misuses.

CHAPTER IX.

THE RECONNAISSANCE TO DWATOI.

"What by duty's voice is bidden, there where duty's star may guide,
Thither follow, that accomplish, whatsoever else betide."

ARCHBISHOP TRENCH.

"To friends a friend; . . .
To foes how stern a foe was he!
And to the valiant and the free
How brave a chief!"

LONGFELLOW.

THE Tirah expedition was not one in which the troops were allowed much rest. On November 18 General Westmacott's Brigade went out foraging, and on the 19th it marched with Sir William Lockhart and his Staff from the camp at Maidan to Bagh. That the troops knew little or nothing of the task awaiting them appears from a remark in a letter from Colonel Haughton, written at Bagh on November 21. "I hear our Brigade is going out to-morrow to a place called Dwatoi, some miles from here; but whether we are going there, only to come back again, is more than I know. I do not mind the going, but do not like the coming back."

Next morning (22nd) a strong force* under

* King's Own Scottish Borderers, 1/3rd Gurkhas, 36th Sikhs, 28th Bombay Pioneers, No. 5 Bombay Mountain Battery, No. 4

Brigadier-General Westmacott, accompanied by Sir William Lockhart, started from Bagh for Dwatoi, the point where the Shal-oba ("twenty streams or springs") river, which drains Maidan, meets with the stream that flows down from the Rajgul valley, which is inhabited by the "Kuki Khel" clan of the Afridis. The united streams are known as the "Bara" river, down the bed or along the banks of which Sir William Lockhart, with Kempster's (3rd) and Westmacott's (4th) Brigades, made his now historical return march towards India. In that march he severed his communications, just as Sir Neville Chamberlain did in 1861 when he made his sixteen days' raid through the Mahsud Waziri country.

We are, however, slightly anticipating events. Of this little expedition to Dwatoi General Westmacott remarked in a letter which he kindly wrote me some months later: "I think where Haughton distinguished himself as much as anywhere was commanding the rear-guard in a very catchy reconnaissance of four days that I made with Sir William Lockhart to Dwatoi." The country between Bagh and Dwatoi was then absolutely unknown. No doubt the intelligence officers had obtained, by questioning natives, some general notion of the nature of the road and its surroundings; but we all know how very vague such information is. It proved to be the most difficult bit of country that

Company Madras, and No. 3 Company Bombay Sappers and Miners, the Gurkha scouts of both divisions, and Field Hospitals.

our troops had to traverse in Tirah; but the fact remains that no reconnaissance in Tirah was carried out with so little loss.

The orders issued for the march were, briefly, these—

"Blankets, greatcoats, and waterproof sheets only (no tents) to be taken. First Reserve Ammunition to accompany the column. One day's supplies to be carried by the troops, two days' in regimental charge (on mules). The Yorkshire Regiment and 1/2nd Gurkhas to move out at 5.30 a.m. and occupy the heights on either side of the Dwatoi defile, Yorkshires on the right, Gurkhas on the left. Advanced guard (1/3rd Gurkhas and No. 4 Company Madras Sappers and Miners) to move off at 6 a.m., followed by the main body (King's Own Scottish Borderers, No. 5 Bombay Mountain Battery, No. 3 Company Bombay Sappers and Miners, and 28th Bombay Pioneers), Field Hospital and Transport, rear-guard, 36th Sikhs."

Our flanking battalions moved off in the dark, and, despite some resistance from the Afridis, won their way to the heights. The ascent was so steep that no mules could follow the Yorkshire Regiment; and the bedding, water, and rations of that corps, having to be sent up by hand, did not reach them till the afternoon of the 23rd. They spent the night of the 22nd in the bitter cold on those cliffs without food or bedding; and, indeed, Sir William Lockhart, General Westmacott, and the troops with them did the same at Dwatoi.* The start of the advanced

* This was no uncommon thing for Sir William Lockhart. I was commanding a company of mounted infantry under him at Yamethen,

guard was considerably delayed, and it was 9 a.m. before the main body, with Sir William Lockhart, marched off. Though the two flanking regiments prevented any massing of the enemy, the march of the column was opposed all day by small bodies from the lower spurs and ridges. The track was most difficult. Bagh itself is situated near the southern outlet of the Shaloba defile, Dwatoi being at the northern end. The distance between the two places is six miles, five of which are in this narrow defile, flanked by precipitous and partially wooded hills. The path is so narrow in places that but one mule could pass at a time, and that only when the Sappers and Pioneers had improved the track. Here and there the path led along ledges on the sides of the cliff, and, clever as mules are, some of them fell over into the stream below and were killed. The water in the stream was two feet deep, and icy-cold, and both troops and transport had to cross and recross it continually throughout the day. The main body reached Dwatoi about 4 p.m. The King's Own Scottish Borderers and 28th Pioneers at once attacked the enemy, who were holding the adjacent hills to the north, and

in Burma, in the cold weather of 1886–87. On one long march of from thirty-six to forty miles, I was detailed for rear and baggage guard. Progress is slow in the Burmese jungles. I left at 10 p.m., and after marching twenty-three hours, found myself, at 9 p.m., in black darkness, at the foot of an impassable ascent. I had to bivouac where I was. Sir William was only a mile or two away on the other side of the ridge, but he and his troops had to pass the night without food or bedding, much to my annoyance at failing to reach them before darkness and the difficulties of the track obliged me to halt.

THE DWATOI DEFILE. (GENERAL WESTMACOTT'S BRIGADE MARCHING THROUGH IT.)

drove them back. Picquets were posted to screen the camp from sniping. The Afridis, however, hung around, waiting for dark to attack the camp and baggage; and desultory firing was kept up. The baggage never came within reach of the expectant foe; for Colonel Haughton, with that intuition which usually prompted him to do the right thing, halted and parked it in the pass for the night. A pleasant spot for a bivouac! Colonel Haughton can best tell his own tale, as he wrote it in the pass itself—

"*November* 22.—We are on rear-guard again, and goodness only knows when we shall get into camp. I believe we return to Bagh the day after to-morrow. I hear a good deal of firing going on in front of us, so suppose the advance is being opposed. We do not mind being opposed in advance, but the nasty job is being followed up when retiring. In European war, under such circumstances, one would just leave one's wounded behind, but, fighting with these ruffians, that would mean death and mutilation to the wounded."

Meantime, the troops at Dwatoi, without either blankets, greatcoats, or food, and wet to the waist, had to go out on picquet duty and get through the night as best they could. There were seventeen degrees of frost. Some anxiety (needless, as it proved) was felt there for the baggage and rear-guard. However, all was well, and about 11 a.m. on the 23rd the first of the baggage and its escort began to arrive. The Pioneers and Sappers had gone back into the pass early, to improve the road as far as time would permit. Meantime, the other troops were destroying the Kuki Khel villages, and the Survey party was busy. About 4 p.m. a strong body of Afridis occupied a hill to the north, and opened an annoying fire on both camp and picquets. Four companies of the King's Own Scottish Borderers, under Colonel Dixon, attacked and dislodged them; but later they crept up under cover of the holly-oak jungle close to the picquets, and kept firing into them until midnight. A bitter cold wind set in at nightfall, but the troops now had food and warm clothing. Colonel Haughton, with the last of his baggage and rear-guard, had come in safe and sound before nightfall. His wayside letter again tells us his experiences.

"*November* 23; 1.15 *p.m.*—Still on the road to Dwatoi, and likely to be till dark. Dwatoi is only about six miles from Bagh. The baggage of our Brigade and the Army Headquarter Staff baggage started yesterday, commencing at about 7 a.m. We (36th) were on rear-guard. At sundown the head of the baggage had got about three and a half miles (so you may imagine what the road was like); so I stopped it all and parked it for the night in a place where there were a few terraced fields on the hillside, put out picquets, and there spent the night. The road in front of us was even worse, so it was impossible to have got any further in the dark. We were comfortable enough, but the troops in front of us had no baggage. This morning we, or rather part of the baggage, started off, my men going on with their picks and shovels and crowbars to try and make some sort of road. I am in hopes that we may get in to-night, as camp is only about two and a half miles distant, and the last mile and a half is comparatively good going. It is mostly a river with a very rocky stony bed, but is like 'Rotten Row' compared to what is before it. I, like most others, got very wet yesterday, fording the river many times; but I was all right, having a complete change of clothes, which many had not. The people generally were fairly peaceable, but there are one or two who have done a lot of sniping, and have hit five or six men. You may say, 'Why don't you stop them?' but, if you saw the country, you would know that it was not so easy. I have sent some men up some fearful hills, and they and the Gurkhas on the other hills seem to have driven the snipers off."

Colonel Haughton's stay at Dwatoi was a very brief one. In fact, we may say that he spent the three days (22nd to 24th November) on rear-guard duty—two days going and one returning. Sir William Lockhart decided on an early move on the morning of the 24th, knowing that the Pathan is loth to act until the sun is up. The camp was astir at 5.30, and so quickly and expeditiously were the sick and wounded, hospitals and transports, got under way, that they were all back into the defile before the Afridis could get a chance of attacking them. They consequently had only the picquets and rear-guard (36th Sikhs as usual) to deal with; and as two guns, posted near the mouth of the defile, covered the retirement of the picquets, which again mutually protected each other, little if any loss was incurred. Colonel Haughton's diary, under date November 25, thus continues his narrative—

"We got into camp at Dwatoi at dusk (on 23rd). It was fearfully cold, eighteen degrees of frost and a horrible wind. I had my 'dog-kennel,' and was fairly snug at night. We had two men wounded during the night by snipers. We got up at 5.30 a.m., but did not ourselves get off till nearly eight, as we were on rear-guard. Things soon began to get lively. It was terribly cold, as, in addition to the wind, the road for the first mile and a half was mostly in the icy water of the river. Then the river takes a sharp turn, and the road (a goat-track) goes up over some rocks on to the hillside above the river. Of course there was a tremendous block here, and the enemy from long ranges, with Lee-Metford rifles, began to snipe us freely. I went on about fifty yards, to try and find positions from which we could fire, etc. While away, out of the four companies behind, three moved off up the hills to turn out some of the enemy. I sent back for a company to come on to me, not knowing that there was only one company there. This came along, and I posted it on a spur overlooking the river by which we had come. The consequence was that there were some thirty hospital ponies and some doolies, etc., down in the river-bed with nobody behind them, though we were on the bank immediately above them, but we could not actually see them. Suddenly there was a shout of 'Pathans!' and almost immediately we saw about thirty Pathans going off up the river (down which we had come) with a dozen ponies. They had crept down under cover of the banks, but were unable to get back that way with the ponies. Some managed to get across, though of these several were hit, but some others took protection under the banks, and apparently dared not face the bit of open they would have had to cross. Or, possibly, they may have thought that we would not come back, and of course, as long as we did not do so, they were quite safe. However, Captain Venour

A TIRAH "DOG-KENNEL."

DWATOI.

(*From a photograph by Lieut.-Colonel John Haughton.*)

(5th Panjab Infantry, doing duty with the 36th Sikhs) went down with a section and attacked them, whilst the rest of the company waited on the top ready to fire if they ran away. Unfortunately they passed one man, who was under the bank, and who fired into them after they had passed, and wounded Captain Venour slightly in the leg, and killed a sepoy before he himself was killed. I then went down, and we went on until we overtook all the ponies. However, three of the ponies were so badly wounded that we had to shoot them. I counted five Pathans dead on the ground, and know there were more hit, but we only got two rifles. Altogether it was a little bit of excitement, and I expect will make the enemy a little more careful about following up. It was a score, as on so many occasions our troops have left dead behind, and the enemy hardly ever do, but on this occasion the process was reversed. It is a treat to get near the enemy, as usually they simply lie hidden at eight hundred yards or so, and snipe one in safety to themselves; and in this way, I am sorry to say, in addition to Captain Venour and the man who was killed, we had thirteen men wounded besides two the night before and one last night. Captain Venour makes the sixth officer who has been wounded with the regiment."

The last of the rear-guard reached the camp at Bagh by 5 p.m. on the 24th. Thus, while the six-mile march to Dwatoi took thirty-six hours (*i.e.* six hours per mile), the return from it, thanks to the work done on the track by the pioneers and sappers, took only ten hours, or two-thirds of a mile per hour. As the rear troops debouched from the defile, the 2nd Yorkshire Regiment, and the 1/2nd Gurkhas simultaneously fell back from the heights commanding the pass. The enemy followed, and kept up a heavy fire on the retiring troops, but there were no casualties. The correspondent of the *Times of India*, writing on the spot and at the time, concludes his account in these words:—

"It was a most masterly retirement, and the whole force is enthusiastic over General Westmacott's handling of his small force, and of the magnificent work of Colonel Haughton and the 36th Sikhs. This is the fifth rear-guard action which they have been called upon to fight during the last month, and on each occasion they have acquitted themselves like men. Six officers have been wounded, and considerably over a hundred men killed and wounded, since the first attack was made on the Samana range. The reconnaissance to Dwatoi from Tirah Maidan deserves to be historical, not only on account of the hardships which the men so cheerily endured, but on account of the magnificent way both the advance and retirement were conducted, the gorge being the worst that any frontier soldier has seen in our frontier wars. While enthusiastic over the troops of the main body, the work done by the Yorkshires and the 1/2nd Gurkhas must not be forgotten. In crowning the flanking heights, they often had to fight detached skirmishes, and two British officers of the Yorkshire Regiment fell while gallantly leading their men. The 2nd Yorkshire Regiment and 1/2nd Gurkhas remained out on the hills three days and two nights. They had a very trying time. Whilst clearing off the Afridis (on the 22nd) two young officers of the Yorkshires (Lieutenant D. E. C. Jones and 2nd Lieutenant O. C. S. Watson), with ten or twelve men, most gallantly turned some of the enemy out of three houses on a spur commanding the ravine. The officers led, and used their revolvers. Lieutenant Jones, just out from England, was killed, and 2nd Lieutenant Watson, with a few months' service only, was dangerously wounded. It is only a few days ago that Major-General Symons * highly complimented two other young officers of this battalion in front of their companies for their dash and courage in leading their men."

* Sir Penn Symons, who died of his wounds after the battle of Dundee (Natal), in October, 1899.

CHAPTER X.

THE MARCH DOWN THE BARA VALLEY.

"When I first joined the army, the idea prevailed that it was the reckless and lawless man that made the best soldier. I have not found it so. When men are partially fed, cold and wet, and their nerves are shaken by shot and shell, it is not the lawless man, but the soldier who has disciplined himself, who responds most promptly and cheerfully to the call of duty, and does what his Queen and country expect of him."—From General Sir George White's speech at the Homes for Working Boys in London, May 21, 1900.

AFTER the reconnaissance to Dwatoi and the Rajgul valley, General Westmacott's Brigade was left at Bagh to rest for a brief period. Sir William Lockhart, however, sorely tried as he was at this time with indifferent health,* did not spare himself. With Brigadier-Generals Gaselee † and Hill he personally carried out the chastisement of the Massuzai and Chamkanni clans. With that my story has nothing to do. We will return to Colonel Haughton, whom, on December 9, we shall find at Dwatoi, writing thus to his wife:—

* His death in March last was deeply regretted by the Indian army. Under him officers and men were proud to serve; for he feared not responsibility, and always "meant business." He understood frontier war as war, and not as a politically-guided procession. Withal, he was loved as well as feared by the frontier tribesmen, as the Afridis showed by the "send-off" that they gave him in the spring of 1898, when peace was at last concluded. Some of those who gave him the "send-off" are represented in the illustration facing p. 222.

† Now Lieutenant-General Sir Alfred Gaselee, K.C.B., commanding the British Forces at Peking.

DWATOI. (*Taken from Rajgul.*)

"Camp Dwatoi, December 9, 1897.

"We have been having a busy time since I last wrote. On the 7th our Brigade left Bagh. We were, as usual, on rear-guard. We now call ourselves 'The Royal Rear-Guards,' as we always have that onerous duty. . . . As soon as the baggage got to the defile there was an awful jam, and many of the poor beasts, in twenty hours—a good part of which time they had been standing in the water—had only got three miles. I was, till after 2 a.m. the next morning, trying to urge on the baggage, and I think most of the regiments, that came on here, got their kits. I then had to give it up, and about 3.30 a.m. I lay down on some soft stones with a bag of atta as a pillow. I had my poshteen on, fortunately, but my pony, with my blanket and poshteen boots, had lost itself in the crowd of transport. However, I slept like a babe for about two and a half hours, and was not really cold, as I had my feet to a fire, and fortunately it was a much warmer night than we have been having. I then got up, had a good swig of rum and hot water, and proceeded to make myself unpleasant to every one with the baggage. Though I had to wade about in the water a bit, I managed to keep tolerably warm, and got everything in here by 1 p.m. on the 8th.

"Fortunately the enemy let us alone. The rascals had destroyed part of the path which we had made when we came here before, otherwise it is possible all our baggage might have got in on the night of the 7th. Some kind officer had considerately sent me a great hunk of tinned beef and bread, or I should have been in a bad way. I had made my report to the General, when I found that Mr. Van Someren (one of our new youngsters) had been ordered to take a company and occupy a hill from which the enemy were sniping. It occurred to me that the poor boy might have rather a nasty job, so, after changing my wet boots, socks, and breeches, and casting a longing look at the tiffin which was getting ready, I got hold of a company and made a detour over some fearful hills, so as to catch the enemy in flank, whilst he was attacking them in front. Mr. Turing asked to come with me, and I was very glad to have him. After I left, the General sent an order for the rest of the regiment to turn out to support Mr. Van Someren's company. I am glad I had not waited for orders, as I believe, without our flank attack, he, although reinforced, would have had a very hard job, and would have lost a lot of men. As it was we had only three men wounded; and a company of the Gurkhas, who had joined Mr. Van Someren, had one man killed, but that was after we had all got up, and been there for some time. It was a hard climb, and I was pretty well fagged when I got back to camp about dusk. I left Mr. Craster and Mr. Van Someren with two companies on the hill, and we built them good sangars before we left. I don't think they were attacked, but the night before a picquet of the King's Own Scottish Borderers were more determinedly attacked than on any previous occasion during this expedition. The enemy tried to rush them three times, but never could get nearer than fifteen yards, and I hope lost pretty heavily, though I know shooting at night, even at close quarters, is very ineffective.

"The King's Own Scottish Borderers are a grand regiment. The General was very pleased with Mr. Van Someren. I believe he really did very well, and the enemy only bolted when he got close up. The enemy were shooting horrid straight, and it was wonderful luck that we had only three men hit attacking the place. Several men had their accoutrements and clothing shot through without being touched, and both Mr. Turing and I were several times hit by stones or splinters of stones knocked up by the bullets. Luckily there were a good many small trees and bushes about, so the enemy seldom got a real good view; but we could not move without a bullet hitting either at our feet, or cutting the branches over or beside us. . . . I am now very fit, and was able to eat a mighty dinner when I got in, and sleep the sleep of the just."

It is not my intention here to write a detailed account of the march down the Bara valley from Dwatoi to General Hammond's camp at Swaikot. As I have mentioned in my preface, five historians have already given their several versions of this now historical march. In a memoir of but one actor in that scene of hard work and hard fighting, there is no call to do more than describe the share that that one actor took in it. With the exception of the letter I have just quoted, nothing written by him has come into my hands. Furthermore, during the last two days of the march Colonel Haughton was too unwell for active duty. Hard work and exposure had been his lot for some three months, and for the moment he succumbed to the strain. He was himself again in a day or two.

To revert, however, to the point where we left him—in the camp at Dwatoi on December 8. On December 9, one hundred rifles of the 36th Sikhs formed part of a column commanded by General Westmacott, and accompanied by Sir William Lockhart, which marched five miles up the Rajgul valley and chastised the Kuki Khel villagers. The northern slopes of this valley were found to be overgrown with ilex, olive, and hollyoak; while more distant peaks and passes were seen covered with snow and pine-forest. On December 10 the march down the Bara valley commenced. Haughton with his regiment formed the advanced guard of the column. The 4th Brigade led the way, and the 3rd Brigade brought up the rear, the transport moving between the two. The weather was bitterly cold, the troops and animals had to wade all day through water, and the enemy hung upon the front, flanks, and rear—especially the rear, of the column. Though no serious loss was sustained, the 3rd Brigade only succeeded in reaching Karana by nightfall, five miles from Dwatoi, and three miles short of Sandana, where the 4th Brigade was encamped. At 7 p.m. rain set in and lasted all night. The troops spent a very miserable night, for all tents had been left behind, and the baggage of the column had been reduced to the minimum. However, when day broke on the 11th, the inevitable march had to be resumed. Wet and weary, troops and followers got under way. The distance from Sandana to Sher Khel was ten miles, and from Karana thirteen. To attempt such a long march on such a day was a very great mistake. Common sense would have suggested to simply close the 3rd Brigade up to the 4th, or possibly move forward a mile or two from Sandana, provided a suitable camping-ground was found.* However, this is wisdom after the event. What with rain, mist, the

* It is at any rate clear that two miles short of Sher Khel there was a suitable camping-ground, for instructions were sent to General Kempster to halt his 3rd Brigade there, if he wished.

steep banks of the stream which had to be ramped, and the slippery state to which the ramps were soon reduced by the traffic on them, the rear-guard of the 3rd Brigade did not leave Karana till 10.15 a.m. The river had risen considerably, and the flanking duties of the leading Brigade were heavy, though no stubborn resistance was offered by the Zakha Khel tribesmen, through whose territory the column was now moving. By 4 p.m. the 4th Brigade had reached Sher Khel. The 3rd Brigade fared less well. The enemy pressed heavily on the Gordon Highlanders, who formed the rear-guard. As the 4th Brigade marched away from the 3rd, the latter had to send out its own flanking parties. The 4th Brigade should have waited on and regulated its pace by the 3rd. It is true that permission was sent to General Kempster to halt his Brigade two miles short of Sher Khel; and that that officer, by deciding not to avail himself of this permission, is directly responsible for what ensued. At the same time we cannot help feeling that the 4th Brigade might have done more to help the 3rd. Major Downman, of the Gordon Highlanders, held that day the responsible post of rear-guard commander, and acquitted himself right well. He fell, two years later, on the field of Magersfontein, fighting staunchly to the last. It has been proved on the most undeniable evidence that the statement that he ordered the retirement of the Highlanders was a complete misapprehension. He jumped up to *stop* a retirement, and was instantly shot dead by the

Boers. This is the evidence of an eye-witness who was at his side.

General Kempster having, most unfortunately, decided to push on to Sher Khel, the transport towards dusk got hopelessly entangled in some rice-fields, three miles short of that camping-ground. The transport drivers, worn out with cold and fatigue, discovered alcohol and made themselves hopelessly drunk. Others deserted their animals and went on to Sher Khel. Major Downman saw the only chance of safety for his tired and belated rear-guard was to occupy and hold some defensive position during the night. He therefore seized a small hamlet, and there, with his men, maintained himself in safety till morning. The Afridis kept up a desultory fire on them, but did not care to come to close quarters. The fascinations of pillaging drew off numbers from the less lucrative amusement of "sniping" at the rear-guard. A very small effort had been made to send back assistance from Sher Khel. One company of the King's Own Scottish Borderers went out and helped in a number of soldiers, followers, and transport animals, as well as a party of wounded, some of whom were being carried in by officers. The manner in which the drivers deserted the animals, and the doolie-bearers the wounded, on this occasion, is a proof—if any proof is needed—of the little reliance that is to be placed on this class of native of India at a pinch.*

* If we had trained Ambulance Corps in India, some *esprit de corps* might be instilled into them, and also such a sense of discipline

LAST AND WORST BLOCK OF BAGGAGE IN THE BARA RIVER AT GALAI KHEL.

When in frontier warfare it is plain that a column cannot reach camp before dark, there is really only one resource, and that is to collect the troops, pack the transport, and remain all night on the defensive. This is what Colonel Haughton did instinctively; and had General Kempster done the same on December 11, the worst mishap of the Bara valley retreat would have been avoided. Early on the 12th General Kempster set out from Sher Khel with two battalions and a mountain battery to endeavour to repair as far as possible the mischief resulting from the mistakes made on the 11th. Many transport animals and followers and many of the loads were never recovered. The rear-guard, under Major Downman, was found completely surrounded by the enemy, who had seized some good positions around the houses, and having at dawn crept up close, had succeeded in killing and wounding several of the Gordon Highlanders. By 11 a.m. this rear-guard had been safely escorted into the Sher Khel camp. A halt for the day had been ordered. The weather was bright and warm, and every one basked in the sun and dried his kit. It is again impossible not to reflect that, had the dictates of common sense been listened to the previous day, and a halt or very short march been ordered, the sad scenes with which the names "Bara valley"

and duty as would prevent this dastardly desertion of the sick and wounded. We ought to have in India a trained Ambulance Reserve such as that which the Order of St. John of Jerusalem placed at the disposal of the British Central Red Cross Committee for South Africa. —*Vide* Appendix C, and Journal of the Royal United Service Institution for October, 1900.

and "Sher Khel" will always be associated, might never have taken place. The casualties on the 11th were: two officers severely wounded, seven men killed, seven men dangerously, twenty severely, and eight slightly wounded.

On December 13, after a most welcome and necessary rest for twenty-four hours, the Division started for Swaikot. (If in this march little or no mention is made of Major-General Yeatman-Biggs, commanding the Division, it must be borne in mind that he was throughout it seriously ill and unfit for duty. He died a few weeks later.) The order of march was now changed. The 3rd Brigade led, and the 4th Brigade brought up the rear. It was on December 13 and 14 that Colonel Haughton was too unwell for duty. The command of the 36th Sikhs devolved on Major Des Vœux. The lessons learnt on the 11th resulted in the issue of orders: (1) that flanking parties and picquets were not to leave their posts until the whole Division had passed; (2) that the advanced guard of the leading and the rear-guard of the rear Brigade were each to consist of half a battalion; (3) that special guards of an officer and twenty men were to be told off to guard each hospital and keep the doolie-bearers to their work.

As a specimen of the arrangement of a column on the march during this Tirah expedition, I may, perhaps, without risk of being tedious (to soldiers, at any rate, who study their profession), state in detail the formation and order of the Division during this, the most critical day's march in the Bara valley. According to the information received, the best route was said to be down the river bed for three miles to a village named Galai Khel. There the track was said to leave the river and follow a narrow valley to the Lakarai Kotal, and after crossing that Kotal to descend to Swaikot, leaving Shinkamar defile (made only too memorable on January 29, 1898) on the left and Barkai on the right. It was reported that there was no water between Galai Khel and Barkai. The troops were warned of this, and ordered to carry water. Shinkamar was supposed to be seven miles from Sher Khel, and was fixed upon as the halting-place. The distance, however, proved to be greatly under-estimated. The 3rd Brigade marched at 7.30 in the following order:—*Advanced guard:* four companies Gordon Highlanders under Colonel Mathias, two guns, and two companies Sappers and Miners. *Flanking parties:* 2nd Punjab Infantry and 2nd Gurkhas. *Main body:* four guns, four companies Gordon Highlanders. *Transport*, with the hospitals in the middle. *Rear-guard:* the Dorset regiment.

This Brigade met with no resistance worth speaking of. The 4th Brigade had a very different experience. It left camp in the following order:—*Advanced guard:* Jhind Infantry. *Hospitals. Transport. Main body:* Royal Scots Fusiliers, 28th Bombay Pioneers, Northampton Regiment, No. 8 Mountain Battery, King's Own Scottish Borderers, 36th Sikhs. *Rear-guard:* No. 5 (Bombay)

Mountain Battery, 1/3rd Gurkhas, Gurkha scouts. This Brigade began to move off at 9.30. The last baggage did not get away till 10.45, and behind that was the main body and rear-guard. A narrow defile in the river-bed three quarters of a mile from the camp delayed the whole column. Much difficulty also was experienced in withdrawing the picquets. The enemy had crept up under cover close to them, and no sooner did they leave their posts than the enemy occupied them and opened fire. No. 5 Bombay Mountain Battery had to come into action to cover the retirement of these picquets, and even then the enemy were actually into the houses of the "Sher Khel" village before the King's Own Scottish Borderers were well out of them. Practically, throughout this march, the entire main body of this Brigade was a rear-guard. The batteries fell back and took up positions successively to cover the troops in rear. The 3rd Gurkhas were in rear of all, with two companies in the river bed and one on each bank. The Gurkha scouts destroyed all fortified villages from Sher Khel to Galai Khel. At the latter place a narrow steep track leads upward from the river-bed towards the Lakarai Kotal. Here, as a matter of course, the baggage was greatly delayed, and the entire Brigade made a long halt. The enemy thought they saw their opportunity, and pushed on by the north side or left flank of the column with the intention of falling on the baggage and cutting in between the two Brigades. The dispositions made by General

Westmacott completely foiled this stratagem. The enemy found themselves under a heavy cross-fire of guns, Maxims, and musketry, and were driven back with a loss estimated at from three hundred to four hundred men. By the time the 36th Sikhs and 1/3rd Gurkhas reached Galai Khel, they had exhausted their pouch ammunition, and had to replenish it from the reserve.

From Galai Khel the track ascended, crossing ridge after ridge covered with prickly scrub jungle. The track was rough and narrow, and two lines of mules could with difficulty march abreast. The column thus strung out to a great length. The retirement was carried out by battalions, which alternately took up successive positions, and covered each other's withdrawal. The enemy never relaxed the rigour of their pursuit, and, as darkness came on, advanced into the open and came to close quarters. General Westmacott, seeing that it was impossible to reach the Lakarai Kotal before nightfall, halted his force for the night on a ridge running right across the line of retirement. The enemy boldly charged this line, and got within a few yards of the King's Own Scottish Borderers and 3rd Gurkhas, but were driven back with heavy loss. Here Lieutenant West of the 3rd Gurkhas was killed. He was an officer who had done good service, and distinguished himself on several occasions during the expedition. The surrounding heights were held throughout the night by the picquets of the 3rd Brigade. The 4th Brigade spent a comfortless night without food, water, and blankets, as their baggage had gone on to the spot where the 3rd Brigade had bivouacked, half a mile west of the Lakarai Kotal. Here a small force from Swaikot, under General Hammond, with eight doolies and three hundred doolie-bearers, joined the column. The doolie-bearers of General Yeatman-Biggs' Division had completely broken down, and for the last two days most of the sick and wounded had been carried by their soldier comrades.

At daybreak on December 14 the retirement recommenced in the same order as on the 13th. The 3rd Brigade met with no opposition, and on arrival at Mamanai, on the right bank of the Bara river, where it encamped, sent back water to the 4th Brigade, which, as far as the Lakarai Kotal, was pursued as vigorously by the Afridis as on the previous day. It was about 10.30 a.m. when the baggage of the 4th Brigade got under way. As on the previous day, the battalions retired successively from position to position, chiefly along the northern spurs, which commanded the route. Once the Lakarai Kotal was passed the pursuit was practically abandoned.

Thus ended the march down the Bara valley, one which, for hardship and hard fighting, has scarce an equal in the annals of frontier warfare. (That which approaches nearest to it is Sir Robert Sale's march from Kabul to Jalalabad in October, 1841.) The casualties were considerable.*

* Casualties: Lieutenant West killed, 7 officers and native officers

On the following day (December 15) Sir William Lockhart issued an order specially complimenting General Westmacott and his troops on the work that they had done; and on December 22 he conveyed to the whole Division the thanks of the Commander-in-Chief in India, Sir George White, and to Brigadier-General Westmacott the Chief's appreciation of his "able generalship and soldierly discharge of his duty."

severely wounded, 31 non-commissioned officers and men killed, 126 wounded (28 dangerously, 68 severely, 30 slightly). The 36th Sikhs had 4 killed and 21 wounded (3 dangerously, 7 severely). On them and the 3rd Gurkhas the brunt of the fighting fell. Lieutenant West was afterwards specially mentioned in despatches, with Colonel Haughton, as one who, had he survived, would have been recommended to Her Majesty for reward.

CHAPTER XI.

REST AND DEATH.

"Greater love hath no man than this, that a man lay down his life for his friends."—ST. JOHN xv. 13.

"No welcome greeted our return
Nor clang of martial tread,
But all were dumb and hushed as death
Before the mighty dead."

AYTOUN'S *Lays.*

THE period which now followed was one of rest for the 2nd Division. It fell to the lot of the 1st Division (Symons') and Hammond's Brigade to overrun the Bazar valley and reoccupy the Khyber. When General Yeatman-Biggs was invalided about December 22, Sir Power Palmer assumed command of the 2nd Division. General Westmacott's Brigade remained encamped at Mamanai; and there it was joined by the 2nd Battalion Yorkshire Light Infantry, sent up to take the place of the Northampton regiment. Nothing of importance happened until the ill-fated, and, as many think, ill-advised raid into the Kajurai plain led to the reverse in the Shinkamar pass, and to—saddest of all—the death of Lieut.-Colonel Haughton and his Adjutant, Lieutenant Turing, men who had faced death and survived danger so often in the last three months, only to lose their lives in a fruitless little foray, just when well-earned rest and reward seemed within their reach. And, indeed, they won their rest and reward —the rest that nothing on earth can break, and, as their heritage of reward, the grief of the Army and the Nation. When the news of Haughton's death spread through India, it is not too much to say that every Englishman's heart mourned for his loss.

In the last few days of his life Colonel Haughton did place on record some of the impressions which the Tirah expedition had made on his mind. In a letter dated January 20, 1898, he says—

"I think much of the criticism in the papers on this campaign has been very unfair. Of course there have been mistakes made (even Napoleon and Wellington made mistakes in every campaign), and though there may be some blame due, it must be remembered that there were great and unusual difficulties. The country was absolutely unknown except from hearsay; it would be very hard to find a more difficult country to operate in; and finally, owing to so many disturbances (in Tochi, Malakand, etc.), there was great difficulty in getting the large amount of transport required, and it was not good when finally obtained. The delay in getting transport delayed the expedition, and consequently we were very much pressed for time, and not able to overrun the country as thoroughly as we otherwise should. I think, too, that things would have gone better had Sir William Lockhart been in better health. To talk of 'disasters' and such-like is ridiculous. The troops did everything possible, and the enemy could never prevent us going where we liked, and doing whatsoever we chose to do. That the enemy would not fight was not our fault, as, with a friendly

Afghanistan close to them, they could always seek safety for themselves, their families, and their cattle across the border."

A much more detailed review than this, written by him on January 16, 1898, to General Sir Charles Gough, I have given in an Appendix (A). Despite all that the Press has written on the subject, this review is the most valuable piece of criticism on the Tirah expedition that has yet appeared in print; for it is written by a man who saw all with his own eyes, who had a very sound judgment, and whose eminent success and known sincerity negatives even the suspicion of an *arrière-pensée*.

I have received accounts of the Shinkamar affair from three or four officers (of different corps) who either took part in it, or were in a position to know very well what did occur. I shall base my account on theirs.

The raid on the Kajurai plain was a combined movement from the four Brigades, the headquarters of which were respectively at Bara, Mamanai, Jamrud, and Ali Masjid. The object was to seize the Afridi cattle grazing on that plain, and drive the Afridis out of it. It was thought that this would have a salutary effect on them. Unfortunately the plan resulted in a complete *fiasco*. We played into the hands of the Afridis. There is very little doubt that they had full information of what was going to be done, and laid their plans accordingly. They removed their cattle and concentrated their whole strength against our small column, with the result which is about to be made known.

On or about January 27 the General Officers commanding the 3rd and 4th Brigades, with their Staff and Political officers, met at Gandao to discuss the projected raid. They each sent in their reports, and in due course orders were received. The 3rd Brigade was at Bara, fifteen miles north-east of the Shinkamar pass, and the 4th at Mamanai, seven miles to the south-east of it. What orders the 3rd Brigade received are of no concern, for the 4th Brigade saw no sign of either that or of the 1st and 2nd Brigades throughout the day. The orders sent to Mamanai on January 28 were, briefly, to send out an adequate force of infantry with guns early on January 29, to occupy the Kotal of the Shinkamar pass by 10 a.m., to examine certain caves in the vicinity of that pass, and communicate, if possible, with the 3rd Brigade column from Bara, and to commence the retirement to camp at 1 p.m. General Westmacott accordingly selected Lieut.-Colonel Seppings, of the King's Own Yorkshire Light Infantry, for the command, with Major Rose, of the 3rd Gurkhas, as his staff officer, and placed the following troops under him :—Two guns No. 5 Bombay Mountain Battery, under Lieutenant Massie; 427 rifles of the Yorkshire Light Infantry, under Major Barter; 200 rifles 36th Sikhs, under Lieut.-Colonel J. Haughton. General Westmacott further sent a detachment of the 3rd Gurkhas out towards the Lakarai Kotal, so as to check any attempt of the Afridis to come in on the left flank and rear of the column, and occupied the hills from west to east on the right of the pass with some of the Bombay Pioneers.

The force under Colonel Seppings started from Mamanai at 5 a.m. on the 29th.* The 36th Sikhs formed the advanced guard under Colonel Haughton. When the foot of the pass was reached, at 7.30 a.m., Afridis were seen retiring up it, driving their cattle before them. These were refugees from the caves on the south side of the pass. A company of the Yorkshire Light Infantry occupied a knoll, and opened fire on the retiring Afridis, while another company was sent to occupy and hold the heights on the right (or east) of the Kotal. At the same time Colonel Haughton detaching one or two of his companies to scale and hold the heights on the left (or west) of the pass, himself led the central attack straight up to the Kotal. No opposition worth speaking of was offered. The guns were left at the mouth of the pass, with half a company of the Yorkshire Light Infantry as escort. It seems that the knoll already mentioned as occupied by a company of the Yorkshire Light Infantry would have made an excellent position for a covering battery; but no such use was made of it. Half

* I find in one report the following remark: "The first error of the day was visible at 9 a.m., when we saw their route marked by burning villages, thereby calling the country to arms. This should have been done, of course, on the way home." What was burnt appears to have been Afridi property found in some caves near the entrance to the Shinkamar pass. A company of the Yorkshire Light Infantry was directed to burn these things about 8 a.m.

a company of the Yorkshire Light Infantry was sent to hold a point halfway up the heights on the left of the pass. The remainder of the Yorkshire Light Infantry was held in reserve behind the knoll.

Such, as far as can be gathered, was the disposition of Colonel Seppings' force between 10 and 11 a.m. No sign was to be seen of any body of troops from the 3rd Brigade. The caves beyond the pass were, if possible, to be visited. Colonel Seppings asked Colonel Haughton by heliograph if he could do so within the time, *i.e.* so as not to delay the retirement beyond 1 p.m. Colonel Haughton at once undertook to do it, and started off, directing his Sikhs to follow him. He did not intend that order to apply to the left flanking company, but that company understood it so, and followed him, and hence arose all the mischief. The enemy saw their chance, seized the height vacated by that company of Sikhs, and thereby got command of the top of the Kotal and therefore of the main line of retreat. It is said that an officer of the Yorkshire Light Infantry, seeing the Sikhs leave their post, foresaw the possible evil result, and suggested that he should take his company up and occupy the height now left defenceless. He was told, however, to stay where he was. Colonel Haughton meantime pushed on (picqueting the heights as he went) to the caves distant from one to one and a half miles, the Afridi men, women, and children stampeding out of them, as he approached.

Having examined them, he commenced his retirement; and though followed up, reached the Kotal with very little loss, to find it completely commanded by the fire of the enemy from the heights on the left. This was about 1 p.m. Colonel Seppings meanwhile, when he saw the Afridis in dangerous force on the heights on the left of the Kotal, sent two companies of the Yorkshire Light Infantry in succession, the first under Lieutenant Dowdall, the second under Lieutenant Walker, to drive them out and reoccupy the heights. This was done, and the Afridis for the time being driven back to the next peak or ridge some two or three hundred yards distant; but Lieutenants Dowdall, Walker, and Hughes were killed, and the two companies so hampered with their killed and wounded, that retirement was only possible by deserting them, and that of course could not for one moment be thought of. The orders which the 36th Sikhs received, on returning from the caves to the Kotal, were to retire and take up a fresh position, so as to cover the subsequent retirement of the Yorkshire Light Infantry. At the same time two fresh companies of the Yorkshire Light infantry were sent to support and extricate the two which were holding the heights on the left of the Kotal. The greater part of the Sikhs fell back, as ordered; but Haughton, followed by Lieutenant Turing and four or five of his men, crossed over the Kotal to the heights on the left, where the Yorkshires were, to help them; for he saw the straits they were in.

When he arrived, the tribesmen were crowding in, around and within a few yards of them.

"He took a Lee-Metford rifle from a Yorkshireman, who was done up, and kneeling down fired a few rounds to keep the Afridis off. About this time Turing was killed, and the few Sikhs with Haughton were either killed or wounded. He still held his ground to cover the retirement of the wounded. His hat was knocked off by a bullet, but he only said, 'That was a near shave,' and turning to Major Barter, told him not to expose himself. Jack was absolutely fearless under fire, and would hardly ever condescend to take cover. He then seems to have been left with very few men, for one of the survivors, a Yorkshireman, reported that Jack, seeing that there was very little hope of successfully retiring, said, 'Now, my men, let us fire a few more shots, then charge the enemy and die like men.' He fired some five more rounds, and then fell dead with a bullet in his brain." *

Such is one account of Haughton's last moments. Another, and from a very reliable source, runs thus :—

"The behaviour of all troops was simply magnificent. Neither officer nor man had any thought of self. They were in a trap, being fired upon from the front and left. Every wounded man was picked up, and very slowly the force worked its way down. Haughton, with his adjutant, Turing, two Sikhs, and two men of the King's Own Yorkshire Light Infantry, got into a commanding position on the left and covered the retirement, the two officers having both picked up rifles and ammunition. Of those two officers and four men, but one (a Yorkshireman) lived to tell the tale. Their ammunition was running out; Turing

* Quoted from an officer's letter.

and the two Sikhs were killed. Haughton told the Yorks lads to fix bayonets, and said, 'We'll shoot away the ammunition we've got, and then show them how British soldiers die.' He was immediately afterwards hit with a bullet in the head, just behind the ear—absolutely painless—and he fell, like the grand soldier and gentleman he was, in endeavouring to save others. One Yorkshireman succeeded in rejoining his corps. The enemy sent the body to Mamanai unmutilated. Few men have served for so short a time as John Haughton had with the Tirah Field Force and so completely won the love and respect, and, I may say, admiration of all of us. In losing him I lost a very dear friend and comrade, and the service lost a brilliant soldier."

To return, however, to the hard-pressed little force. Colonel Seppings, when he saw the difficulties of his position, at once heliographed to Mamanai, and got a prompt reply that General Westmacott was on his way to help him. The retirement went on gradually. Not a wounded man was abandoned. Some dead had to be left, but their rifles and ammunition were carried away. We may well ask, "What, all this time, were the two guns doing?" They are not even mentioned in one of the six printed and four manuscript accounts of this action that are before me. They seem to have been badly posted at first, and to have been of very little use. When the enemy were firing so close on our troops as to be almost intermingled with them, the guns dare not fire. The commanding position held by the enemy on the left compelled the Yorkshire Light Infantry to leave the usual route, and to retire across a succession of knolls on the right of the pass. The one and a half companies of that regiment which had been originally posted to guard the pass held their positions to the end and covered the retirement. Below, in the plain at the mouth of the pass, a position was taken up—presumably by the 36th Sikhs and two guns—through which the parties of the Yorkshire Light Infantry, carrying and guarding the wounded, passed; and to their aid arrived General Westmacott, about 4 p.m., with two guns, two hundred King's Own Scottish Borderers, and one hundred of the 3rd Gurkhas. By 4.30 the last of the troops had been extricated from the pass, and the whole column then fell back slowly on Mamanai, General Westmacott himself, as usual, being with the rearmost troops. Once in the open, the Afridi pursuit slackened. Camp was reached at 7 p.m. The 36th Sikhs were brought out of action by Second-Lieutenant Van Someren, who, on this as on other occasions, proved himself a fine young soldier.

Except in that one struggle to the bitter end, in which Colonel Haughton, Lieutenant Turing, and two sepoys fell, the losses of the 36th Sikhs were trifling. The brunt of the fighting fell on the Yorkshire Light Infantry; and new as they were to the work, they bore themselves most manfully. They lost, in addition to the three officers already mentioned as killed, Major Earle, Captain Marrable, and Lieutenant Hall wounded, twenty-six men killed, and thirty-two men wounded. A soldier made prisoner by the Afridis on this occasion was subsequently returned uninjured, as Sergeant Walker, who was made prisoner during the Bara valley march, had also been.

General Westmacott decided not to take any active steps to recover the dead on January 30, as he did not consider the force at his disposal sufficient. He determined to make a private effort to recover the bodies of Colonel Haughton and Lieutenant Turing. A little incident that had happened a week before contributed to this end. It chanced that a party of Gurkhas had ambuscaded some Pathan "snipers," killed one of them, and captured the body. General Westmacott put the body in a doolie just as it was, and sent it with all respect to the nearest Afridi village, to be handed over to the relations of the deceased. He at the same time sent a message to the effect that this is the way we always treated the dead, and the way they ought to be treated. This judicious act bore good fruit, as will be shown. On January 30 the Political officer attached to General Westmacott's Staff sent some of his men out to the Afridis, and said that General Westmacott was very anxious that the dead should be respected, and above all, that the body of Colonel Haughton should be treated with the honour that so brave a soldier deserved. The Afridis, remembering with gratitude, as we have good reason to believe, the respect with which General Westmacott had treated their dead, placed the body of Colonel Haughton (also that

MONUMENT IN PESHAWAR CEMETERY.

of a British soldier, mistaking it for that of Lieutenant Turing) on a charpoy, and sent it in to Mamanai camp. It was sent into Peshawar the next day, and was buried on January 31 with full military honours in the cemetery there, every officer off duty in the garrison attending; for all wished to do him honour. Over his grave now stands the monument erected to him by his brother officers of the 35th and 36th Sikhs. Just a year after his death some verses appeared in the *Pioneer* to his memory, and to the honour of those who fought with him. I have given them in an Appendix (B).

On January 31 General Westmacott, having received reinforcements from Bara, took out a strong force and brought in twenty-two dead. Not one body had been mutilated. The Afridis made some resistance, and, as usual, followed up the retirement. There were a few casualties.

As far as the 36th Sikhs were concerned, the Tirah expedition was now at an end. On the Samana that regiment had lost one British officer (Lieutenant Blair) * very severely wounded, twenty-one men killed, and one native officer and forty-five men wounded. During the operations in Tirah it lost two British officers killed and seven wounded, fifteen men killed and fifty-seven wounded.

* "At Satara, on the 29th July, 1900, of cholera, Captain A. K. Blair, 36th Sikhs, when employed on Famine Duty. (Deeply regretted by all ranks of his regiment.)"—Obituary Notice in *Pioneer Mail*, August 10, 1900.

CHAPTER XII.

L'ENVOI.

> "If chance thy house
> Salute thee with a father's honoured name,
> Go, call thy sons, instruct them what a debt
> They owe their ancestors."
>
> AKENSIDE.

"*Salus populi suprema lex.* A nation such as ours, nurtured in freedom, ought to rouse itself."—DR. WARRE, at the R.U.S.I., June 27, 1900.

"Next to the pain I felt when one of my sons was rejected for the army, one of the saddest moments of my life was when the time came for my own superannuation."—Remark of a Swiss officer quoted by MR. G. G. COULTON, *National Review*, July, 1900, p. 842.

WITH the experiences and memories of the South African War so present in the minds of all, it is difficult to carry readers back even to so recent a campaign as that of 1897–98 against the Orakzais and Afridis of Tirah. Yet so close, from certain points of view, are the resemblances between the incidents of the several wars and expeditions in which her Majesty's forces have been engaged during the last half-century—while, on the other hand, they are marked by wide distinctions of country, climate, and circumstance—that comments and criticisms suggested by one are often equally applicable to the others. If time and opportunity enabled us to carry back our studies of national warfare and national thought and feeling to the days of the Saxon and Dane, of the Conquest, and of the wars with France and Scotland, we should find, if not "the man in the street," at all events peer and prelate, knight and burgher, artisan and peasant, discoursing on "the lessons of the war." In those days there was no "Daily Press." It is the nineteenth century, with its steam, electricity, and universal education, that has fostered the habit of focussing public opinion in a leading article. The *rôle* of military critic is only one of the many that the versatile journalist of to-day is, often with a minimum of qualification, ready to assume at a moment's notice. Could he in that *rôle* only call into play that journalistic faculty which Lord Curzon of Kedleston once so happily termed "the intelligent anticipation of events before they occur," he would be an invaluable auxiliary of the Intelligence Department, and of every General in the field. Unfortunately his is the belated and dogmatic wisdom that follows the event.

"The lessons of the war" has become a stock expression. The accepted popular belief is that these "lessons" are to be taken to heart by the War Office and the Army alone. They are applicable, rather, to the great British Public itself; for with it largely rests the making of the Army. It is in the lack of education and training, as well as in the prejudice or indifference of the people, that certain causes of defect in our troops are inherent.

Popular feeling has till to-day been averse to a National Army, and the popular life has for decades been no school for soldiers—least of all for the soldiers that the Empire now requires, soldiers who can serve and fight in any clime, against any foe, and under any conditions. And if we may believe Philip de Commines, this same unreadiness and these same causes thereof were as inherent in the English people of the fourteenth and fifteenth centuries as they are in the British Nation of to-day. The pride with which we, whether individually or as an Empire, look back, be it for centuries or for decades, on the military skill and prowess of our ancestors, will always be tempered by the sense of the mistakes that were made. That is inevitable—alike for the past, and for future generations. The South African War promises to do more to remove some of these defects than all the efforts of experts, theorists, critics, and reformers, be they statesmen, soldiers, or journalists, during the last half-century. We are now within a measurable distance of becoming a "Nation in Arms." The country is alive to the need of a more or less universal military education; and a scheme of Army reorganization based on that principle, and having in view home defence, may be reasonably anticipated, provided the opportunity is not let slip. The foreign ill-will which this war has evoked should be a warning to the Nation to make itself strong for defence; and, as every soldier knows, defence means power of offence. In July, 1900, we had about three hundred thousand men fighting on foreign shores, at an average distance of some five thousand miles from their base. The known history of the world records no such feat. It is a proud thought, but again the caution "lest we forget" looms before us. As the South African War has laid bare our defects in military training, in mobility, intelligence, and scouting, and in capacity for home defence, so Tirah taught us that our youth, born and bred in towns and plains, are no match, without proper training and development, for mountaineers. This, from the military and national points of view, and apart from questions of organization and equipment, is the pith of the lessons learnt in Tirah and South Africa.

Dr. Warre's lecture at the Royal United Service Institution on June 27, and the keen comment to which it gave rise both in the Press and on Public School Speech-days, marked, there is reason to believe, an era in the military education of the country. It may be that the Head-master of Eton elaborated his scheme overmuch, but in principle it is sound, and (as he himself stated) approved by eighty-three of the hundred and two members of the Conference of Head-masters. It met with a very favourable reception at the Royal United Service Institution. Fears of War Office interference, and lest "public schools become public camps," have been expressed, but do not appear to be well founded.

The keynote of the Public School Speech-days

in 1900 has been pride in the number of old boys that each School has sent to serve the Empire in South Africa, in China, and in Ashantee.*

That pride has not been least, or with least cause, displayed by the two Schools, Shrewsbury and Uppingham, with which, specially and appropriately, I have been privileged to associate this book. A cadet corps two hundred strong paraded at Uppingham on the speech-day of 1900; and Shrewsbury means to have its own corps at an early date. May both Schools be fruitful of good soldiers † in the future as they have been in the past!

* It is a pride that animates high and low, and which public schools share with the humbler scenes of primary education. When the Duke of York, in July last, opened the Poor Law Schools Exhibition, he stated, amid loud applause, that 361 old Poor Law School-boys were serving their country in South Africa. When military training in public schools is advocated, let us bear in mind that it is none the less necessary and useful in primary schools, Board, Voluntary, or Poor Law. Not the least argument in support of this military training in all boys' schools is the employment that it will afford to retired non-commissioned officers and soldiers of good character. The Duke of York's and Royal Hibernian Schools are examples of what discipline and drill, combined with ordinary education, does for boys.

† Major Sir Claude MacDonald, as already stated in the Preface, is an old Uppingham boy. A year that has witnessed the defences of Kimberley, Ladysmith, and Mafeking, must not forget that of Peking. The three first waged war in a fair and open field, with an enemy that conformed to most of the recognized conventions of civilized war. The last faced a foe that knew no mercy, its sole defence a wall, hemmed in on all sides but one by Chinese dwellings, and commanded by the great wall of the city at a range of a few hundred yards. The British Legation at Peking was as indefensible as the Gurkha barracks at Charikar. In it that brave soldier and staunch diplomat, Sir Claude MacDonald, kept the Chinese hordes at bay for weeks, while the Concert of Europe trifled with the lives of their envoys and their escorts. At the end of March, 1898, the day after Russia occupied Port Arthur, I dined at the Legation at Peking. Dr. Morrison, the well-known and capable correspondent of the *Times*,

Some knowledge of practical soldiering is in these days essential for every citizen. Into whatever line of life a youth may go—Politics, Science, Law, Medicine, Commerce, Journalism, not to mention the Army and the Navy (naval brigades take part frequently in operations on land)—that knowledge will stand him in good stead. The power of the pulpit, also, will profit by it. It should be specially noted that in the South African War the casualties among the officers have, in proportion to the numbers engaged, been nearly three times as great as those among the non-commissioned officers and men. We look to our Public Schools to prepare for the service of the nation a strong Reserve of Officers, sufficient to replace the heavy losses which experience teaches us to expect in our future wars.

The question has been raised whether military training in Public Schools should be compulsory or voluntary. In the Middle Ages the athletic and martial education of the youth of the land was all-important. "Letters" were of little account. To-day the literary and athletic training is well maintained; the martial has fallen into neglect. The curriculum of a Public School is not arranged by the authorities in consultation with parents; but it is so framed as to meet the views and wishes of parents

and Lieut.-Colonel G. F. Browne, Military Attaché, were of the party. After dinner Sir Claude brought out and showed us the original of General Gordon's last telegram from Khartoum. We little thought, as we examined it with keen interest, that before the century had closed the name of Claude MacDonald would have so narrowly escaped being written side by side with that of Charles Gordon on the roll of England's political martyrs.

regarding the education of their sons. The best and final test of soundness of system is popularity. Military training appears to be at the present time popular, both with masters, parents, and boys. There is, then, no obvious reason for placing martial on a different footing from literary and athletic education.

The needs of the age demand a "Nation in Arms." Such is every Continental Nation; none more so than the Swiss, whose National Schools sow the seeds of drill and discipline, and amongst whom to be rejected for military service is a disgrace.*

In Great Britain (as, indeed, in other countries), the need for a military education has a twofold bearing. Firstly, every citizen should be qualified to render the State military service. Under Spartan rule the man unfit to do that was deemed unworthy to live. In this less exacting age physical unfitness frees a man from the obligation to serve, but, in Switzerland at least, rightly imposes the obligation to pay. We suffer in Great Britain from the burden of a class known as the "unemployed;" a class that neither works nor pays, and which is by no means confined to the "submerged tenth." On such some form of National Service, personal or pecuniary, should be made compulsory.

Secondly, there are in the country two classes, who are recruited very largely from the ranks of our Public Schools, to whom some practical knowledge

* *Vide* "A Strong Army in a Free State," by G. G. Coulton, p. 38; and *National Review*, July, 1900, p. 842.

of military training and history is of the highest importance. These are our statesmen and our journalists. I include under the term "statesmen" all who adopt politics as a profession or as a pastime, and under the term "journalist" all who wield the pen. The name of the latter is legion, and their responsibility great. In that they undertake to guide and form the opinion of the people, they ought to possess some adequate knowledge of one of the most vital of the many subjects with which they are called upon to deal, viz. the military history, power, and organization of the empire. It is this knowledge, as well as the technical instruction that a soldier requires, that our Public Schools may with advantage endeavour to inculcate in the youth of the country; and no one surely will contend that, in laying the foundation of this knowledge, they are stepping outside their sphere. Of the military and naval history of his own country (not so much of Greece and Rome) every schoolboy should acquire some general notion; while in the discipline of military training we have an instrument of physical, mental, and moral culture such as few, if any, other branches of instruction afford.

The conditions of modern civilized life leave more or less undeveloped those instincts and habits of "outdoor" or "open-air" observation and deduction, and that resourcefulness in emergency, which it is imperative that a soldier should cultivate and acquire. In men of sporting proclivities these qualities are to some extent developed, as Colonel

Alderson has pointed out. What the Pathan learns on his mountain-side, the Boer on his veldt, the Colonial on the ranche, the prairie, or the cattle-run, the Red Indian and the backwoodsman in the Far West, and the savage in every part of the world—that we must endeavour to inculcate in our youth by deliberate education, seeing that the everyday life of Old England does not call those qualities into play.* There appear to be two ways of doing this, viz. by books and by practical outdoor training. The books that suggest themselves are: Baden-Powell's "Aids to Scouting;" † the works of Francis Parkman and Fenimore Cooper, "Robbery under Arms," "Geoffrey Hamlyn," and other good Colonial books; "Sale's Brigade in Afghanistan," by Chaplain-General Gleig; "Indian Frontier Warfare," by Major G. F. Younghusband; "Savage Warfare," by Captain Peach; Mr. Fitchett's works; and the memoirs of Harry Lumsden, John Jacob, John Nicholson, Herbert Edwardes, Reynell Taylor, Henry Lawrence, Colin Campbell, Sydney Cotton, David Ochterlony, and other famous Indian soldiers. The knowledge of others will enable them to greatly extend this list, to which must also be added some of the recognized manuals of military instruction. The outdoor training will consist in the practical application of the knowledge inculcated in these and similar books. No comprehensive study of the

* See Note A at end of chapter.

† Army headquarters in India took (in July, 1900) two thousand copies of this book and distributed it to the corps in the Indian command.

experiences and lessons of the many wars and expeditions in which the British army has been engaged during the past century or more exists. Such a work, well written, is a *desideratum*. The enemies against whom we have fought since the days when a few hundred French Canadians and American Indians defeated and half destroyed General Braddock's brigade near Fort Duquesne on the Alleghany have taught our Generals and our troops many stern and salutary lessons. Red Indians, Gurkhas, Sikhs, Maoris, Zulus, and Soudanese, as well as Pathans and Boers, have taught us to more than respect their martial qualities, their mobility, courage, *élan*, skill, astuteness, cunning, and energy. The Afridis in Tirah proved themselves adepts at guerilla warfare; for, while incessantly harrying our troops, they rarely, if ever, exposed themselves to heavy loss. It is true that we penetrated and laid waste their country, but at a cost of life more serious to ourselves than to them. If it is a question of the honours of the war, we must in fairness confess that they were divided. It was not our policy to annex Tirah. It remains independent. Our supremacy in South Africa was, on the other hand, essential to the stability of our empire. We had both to subjugate and annex. The task was not accomplished without numerous checks, surprises, and reverses, each one of which, if studied, has its lesson to teach. It was a nation of mounted infantry that taught us these lessons.*

* Vide *National Review*, July, 1900, p. 818, *et sqq.*; and the *Weekly Times* of March 30, 1900.

If the military education of the youth of the country leaves something to be desired, so too does the internal system of training in the Army. For a few years in the seventies the results of a petty and carelessly conducted examination were allowed to deprive young officers of one or two years' service absolutely. That injustice worked its own condemnation in five or six years; but the reign of examination is still supreme. Does it justify itself? The Staff College is held to represent the highest standard of military education in the British Army, and the graduate of that college is regarded as a man marked for special or Staff employ. Now it is permissible to say that the experiences of Tirah and South Africa have not justified the pretensions of the Staff College to be regarded as *par excellence* the training school of the Army for high command in the field. Theoretical education is of no avail if the recipient is not qualified to apply it practically. The perfection of desk-work will not make a soldier or a General. One of the most undesirable features of the system of examination for entrance to and promotion in the Army is its association with "cramming." The War Office would do well to discourage as far as possible army crammers. They do no good to the Army, rather the reverse.*

Whatever faults may be found with our military system and the conduct of our wars, the fact remains that no other power in the world could have put

* See Note B, p. 220.

240,000 men into South Africa and kept and fed them there. This is a powerful answer to any criticism. Many writers seem to assume the hypothesis that perfection of system and of generalship is attainable. The conception of a perfect army and perfect organization and leading is purely academic and utopian. The path of reform is no doubt paved with aspirations after the ideal; but it is practical and usually bitter experience that works reform. If any Englishman conceives that "Mistake in War" is a monopoly of British generalship, let him read a paper under that title by Lieut.-Colonel F. N. Maude, in *Cornhill* for April last. Its few pages are more eloquent and convincing than the columns of comment and criticism which appeared in the Press during and after Tirah, and during the war in South Africa. Happily, amid all that varies, and invites armchair criticism, one thing, by the consensus of all opinion, remains constant—viz. the courage and devotion to duty of the British soldier. South Africa, the Soudan, and Tirah have alike proved it. If South Africa has had some touches of the "picnic" about it, Tirah had none. It was from first to last the stern reality of war. In *Blackwood's Magazine* for last May (p. 742) is quoted an expression of opinion by the late Commander-in-Chief in India, and General Commanding the Forces in Tirah, Sir William Lockhart, which harmonizes most thoroughly with the pride that the Nation feels in the Army which has not only established British supremacy in South Africa, but has also shown the world what the military and maritime power of the British Empire can do. The opinion is this: "What gave me the greatest satisfaction is the proof the Tirah expedition afforded that the British soldier can fight as well as the British soldier fought in the Crimea and the Peninsula."

These, among the last words written or spoken by Sir William Lockhart, require no comment; they speak for themselves.

The year 1900 has removed from our midst two men who have figured prominently as frontier soldiers during the last half-century; both Scotchmen, both winners of the blue riband of the Indian Service, the Commander-in-Chief-ship in India. I speak of Sir Donald Stewart and Sir William Lockhart. The bâton of field-marshal, left vacant by Sir Donald Stewart's death, has passed to another Indian officer of unequalled fame on the frontier, Sir Neville Chamberlain. The memoirs of these three distinguished soldiers, if written and well written, will constitute a history of North-West frontier warfare for the last half-century. The memoir that I now bring to an end is the record of but one expedition, and of the career of one comparatively junior officer. I have written it in the firm conviction that the memory and example of Colonel Haughton deserve to be remembered and kept alive in the Army. To those who knew him best, he was a valued friend; to those whom he commanded, a trusted leader. What a comparative stranger thought of him may be gathered from this letter, written by General Lord Methuen in September, 1899, to a relative of Colonel Haughton—

"He struck me as one of the finest-looking men I have ever seen, and his charm of manner never seemed to leave him. His coolness under fire and the manner in which he exposed himself was the admiration of every one, and, I am quite certain, must have influenced the Afridis as well as ourselves. I can say no more, except that his end was full worthy of his life."

It would be most interesting to know from the lips of the Afridis themselves what impression Colonel Haughton did make on them. His commanding stature, his coolness, his bravery, the charmed life which (like Skobeleff) he seemed to bear, the capacity and resource which foiled their tactics,—these must have impressed them. What he was to the men whom he commanded, we know. His name will long be remembered by the regiment that he commanded and by the Sikhs generally. He seems to have in some degree possessed, like John Nicholson and John Jacob, qualities which engender in the hearts of the natives of India a feeling stronger than love and respect—a spirit of worship. The close of this nineteenth century has set before the public memoirs of these three men, each a man of mark, each bearing the same time-honoured Christian name. From a study of the characters and careers of this trio, the officers of the Indian Army may learn, if not the whole, at least the best part of the duty of a good soldier. John Nicholson was deified in the Panjab in his lifetime.

His grave at Delhi is still a place of pilgrimage. John Jacob broke the power of the Baluch on the Sind Border. He died at Jacobabad in 1858, and is buried there. To his tomb come the descendants of the men he chastised, to pray and invoke his spirit. The grave of John Haughton at Peshawar will, it is safe to predict, be a spot sacred in the eyes of the warriors of the Khalsa, above all of those serving in the 35th and 36th Sikhs. His was an upright, brave, and honourable life, as was that of his father before him, as were also those of his two brothers, Richard and Henry. There can be no more valuable legacy to posterity than such an ancestral record, no better example to the Army than the careers of such men.

NOTE A (to p. 214). A few instances best illustrate my meaning. In Burma in 1886 I was in command of an advanced guard. I came on tracks that suggested the proximity of the enemy. I started back to inform the officer commanding the column, but before I could reach him the "advance" was sounded on a trumpet. The enemy (Kemmendine Prince and his following) escaped us, naturally.

2. On another occasion a column was sent by a detour to surprise and attack a strong body of Burmese. The officer in command (a Lieut.-Colonel) allowed his troops to burn all the deserted villages *en route*. The enemy, it is needless to say, was not surprised.

When officers, some reckoned "smart" officers, make such astonishing blunders as these, it is obvious that some counteracting education is needed.

NOTE B (to p. 216). Efforts are sometimes made (vide *Times*, 22nd August last) to extol "cramming" at the expense of Public School teaching. The Nation, however, knows that our Public Schools are to be relied on to give a sound and healthy education, moral, mental, and physical. "Cramming" is a hot-house system, enervating to the brain, and unimproving to the mind. It is a mere stimulant. Public School education is food and tonic combined.

APPENDIX A.

Letter written by Lieut.-Colonel Haughton to General Sir Charles Gough, V.C., G.C.B., etc.

Camp Mamanai, January 16, 1898.

My dear Sir Charles,

Many thanks for your letter and kind congratulations on the performances of the 36th Sikhs. To me, who have waited impatiently for nearly twenty-six years for a chance of service, it is indeed gratifying to have had command of the regiment in a fairly hot campaign. It has undoubtedly been a trying campaign, but, when one looks back to what you veterans of the Sikh wars and Mutiny did in the way of fighting and marches, then we see that, so far as fighting is concerned, ours has been by comparison mere child's play.

I cannot say that I have seen anything of your son, though I met him once, not knowing that he was your son. His Brigade has been separated from us a good part of the time, and when camped near us, we did not see much of other Brigades in so large a camp.

You are kind enough to say you would like to hear something of my experiences and views, so you must not blame me if I bore you. As regards policy, one wants to be behind the scenes really to judge, yet of course any one who thinks cannot help coming to some conclusion, though such conclusion may be worthless. However, having been on the Samana amongst the Orakzais for a year, I had perhaps more opportunities of forming an opinion than many others. I don't think the present disturbances can be put down to any one cause, and myself I do not think the so-called "forward policy" is mainly responsible. There is no doubt that, amongst other causes, the Greek defeat by the Turks had a good deal of effect, and was used by unscrupulous persons to stir up disquiet. From letters found in a Mullah's house in Tirah, it appeared that the Afridis believed, or at any rate were told, that the English had been beaten by the Turks—that the Russians also had gone against us, and that the Suez Canal was blocked, and we could not get any troops through. I believe myself that, without any direct action, our friend the Amir was not sorry that we should have a thorn in our sides, and also was not sorry that the Afridis should get punishment for not having responded to his claim to be their suzerain, and consequently he connived at their being egged on by the Afghans, notably by the Sipah * Salar. Although the Afridis and Orakzais are not particularly religious, and have themselves said that the tales spread by the Mullahs are all "Mullayani durogh," *i.e.* Mullahs' lies, yet, given any feeling of disquiet, the elder men cannot withstand the Mullahs, backed by the young bloods who are generally spoiling for a fight. I think, with the Mullahs, it was not only fanaticism, but also a desire not to be cut out by each other. Thus the Haddah Mullah, who had been looked on as the leading man in his part of the world, found himself quite eclipsed by the Mad Fakir, and at once set to work to restore his own prestige. In like manner Mullah Syed Akbar and others found themselves being left behind, and so tried to restore their dwindling fame. Then again

* Ghulam Haidar Khan, commanding the Amir's forces on the north-eastern frontier of the Amir's territory.

AFRIDI JIRGAH AT JAMRUD, JANUARY, 1898.

there was seditious incitement from India, when we had allowed sedition to be openly preached, and I fear it is an undoubted fact that there are seditious societies who take any and every opportunity to stir up ill-will against us. In short, as it was no one thing which caused the Mutiny, so, in this case, there were a great variety of factors at work in giving rise to the disturbances on the frontier.

I do not think the Orakzais, or at any rate the greater part of them, ever had their hearts in it, but were dragged in by the Mullahs and by the Afridis. On the Samana we only had half a battalion distributed in seven posts spreading along eight miles of crest. Nevertheless, if we had had a couple of mountain guns, we could not only have completely held our own, but thrashed the enemy had they come on the Samana, which I doubt whether they would have done. Saragarhi, certainly, was a rotten little post, but I must confess that I did not expect it to be regularly attacked in the way it was, as I did not think the enemy would consider its capture worth the great loss they were bound to and did suffer. A great deal has been said about Saragarhi, and, as far as pluck goes, no one could have done more than the poor fellows who fought to the last gasp; but, personally, I think much more highly of the sortie from Gulistan, which was worthy of the best traditions of the Sikhs and of the Indian army. I think Government have made a mistake in having delayed giving a single reward for that. I consider every one of the sortie party should have got the order of merit, and that as soon as possible. Doubtless Government will give some orders of merit, but *bis dat qui cito dat* is a good motto with soldiers and natives, and some recognition would have been very encouraging to the regiment in the subsequent expedition.

As regards the Tirah expedition, I think there has been much very unfair criticism in the Indian papers. At the same time, I think the general impression in the force is that things would have been better managed had Sir W. Lockhart not been in such bad health. He has constantly been down with fever, etc., and I believe has really been ill all the time.

The astonishing and blood-curdling accounts that one sees in some of the home papers would be very amusing, if one did not know that they made one's people at home anxious. On this show (I mean the Tirah in contradistinction to the many others of which I cannot speak) the native troops and the Indian Generals have certainly shown up well on all occasions. . . .

Nothing could have been better or finer than some of the British regiments, especially the King's Own Scottish Borderers and the Gordons. . . . Throughout the expedition we have always gone where we wanted and done whatever we chose to do. But thanks to the guerilla tactics of the enemy, and to their being so well armed (especially with Lee-Metfords taken from British troops), our losses have been out of all proportion to the amount of actual fighting; but it is difficult to see how this could have been avoided. I don't think the Afridis have really played their game at all well. Supposing guerilla tactics were the best, they might have done infinitely more damage to our convoys, which, especially at first, were not well managed; but, judging by Dargai, I doubt if guerilla tactics were their best game. Thanks to the nature of the country, they might have played Dargai over a dozen times, and, as far as we can learn, their losses were trifling at Dargai, whereas we could not have stood that sort of thing repeatedly. Of course, whenever we moved, if even only to get forage, we had a small rear-guard action on the way back, and this perpetual retiring before the enemy was very trying, and I think demoralizing to our troops.

I must confess that hitherto I had always regarded the

Gurkha as rather overrated. I have quite changed my opinion. The 3rd Gurkhas in this Brigade have simply been splendid. Of course I can't say whether the other regiments of Gurkhas are as good, but the 3rd are a grand lot. They have, I think, had an exceptionally good lot of officers, but the men are real good stuff. I think people are apt to forget the change that has taken place in the conditions of frontier fighting. Not many years ago, for instance, in a case like the march down the Bara valley, the baggage would have been quite safe; that is to say, the enemy could not have attacked it without coming down from the hill, and thereby exposing themselves. Now the enemy, with Lee-Metfords and smokeless powder, make it very uncomfortable in the valley from the tops of hills up to eighteen hundred yards on either side; and as we could not see them, and, thanks to the smokeless powder, could not even see where they were, neither our rifle nor artillery fire could do much against scattered small groups. Of course, heights ought to be and were crowned; but, with an enemy armed with modern rifles, this entailed going great distances, and crowning distant heights which, under former conditions, might have been ignored. The work of the advanced and rear guards was enormous, and the enemy, being as active as cats and knowing the ground, enabled a few men with magazine rifles to make it very hot for any party coming to crown a height; and, of course, by the time the party got to the top, with possibly several casualties, not a sign of the enemy was to be seen, till a vicious "phit-phit" or two of a Lee-Metford told you he was on another height half a mile away. I believe the enemy own to a loss of one hundred and sixty on the 13th and 14th of December, and I fancy their loss was a good deal more.

Among several points that have impressed me forcibly are, firstly, the value of *esprit de corps;* and secondly, that in a British regiment, as well as in a native regiment, almost everything depends on the officers. I was also very much struck with the unfitness to march of most regiments, especially British regiments, at the beginning of the campaign. Of course, at the end of the hot weather, there is some excuse for this, but not in the case of regiments that have been quartered in the hills.

I think the King's Own Scottish Borderers and the Gordons had benefited much by the Chitral campaign, although there was so little fighting in it. . . .

Now I will finish this scrawl, which is, I expect, more than you bargained for when you asked me to write.

Hoping you are well and having a good time,

I am, dear Sir Charles,

Yours sincerely,

J. HAUGHTON.

APPENDIX B.

"SHINKAMAR—JANUARY 29, 1898."

Five miles to west we saw the spreading jaws
Of that dread defile, Shinkamar's dark pass,
Whither at dawn of day the little band,
Four hundred hardy dalesmen, Yorkshire's best,
And half their tale of Sikhs, the Khalsa's pride,
Threaded their rocky way. 'Twas now full noon,
And in the busy camp slow whispers passed—
"They marched at five, they should be back by one.
What's the last message? Is there any news?
What says the general?" So the day wore on.
Lining the wall, we stood with straining eyes,
And each man asked his fellow what he saw.
Then came the distant helio's fitful flash:
"Entangled in the nullah—can't get out;
Cumbered with wounded, and they press us close;
We hold our own, but hardly—send us help."
Sudden the bugle blared, the camp uprose,
To arms the Borderer and the Gurkha sprang,
And he, their leader in full forty fights,
First in attack and rearmost in retreat,
Led now the way. Too late, alas! Too late!
Scarce had the common rallying-point been reached,
When the curt message, flag-sent, came to hand,
And silent men learnt how John Haughton died.
"Some one had blundered," and the keen-eyed foe,
Quick to attain the vantage-point in flank,

Pressed on, a hidden host. With grim intent
The veteran Sikh the oft-fought fight renewed,
The stubborn Tyke in dogged silence met
His baptism of fire. Still undismayed
The rear-guard stood, for Haughton bade them stand,
And Haughton's voice to each fresh courage gave,
And Haughton's heart each doubtful breast inspired,
And Haughton's self ten times a hero proved.
Vain the attempt! Swarming on every side,
With hard-won rifle and with rude jezail,
From every rock the howling tribesmen poured.
Swift came the end. 'Twas thus that Haughton died,
And with him Turing, standing by his chief.
But not in vain: respited by the stand,
Slowly and wearily the column reached
The open plain and safely, and the foe,
Baulked of their savage lust, turned to the spoil.
So died John Haughton: by the camp fire's gleam
White men and black their common grief outpoured.
England had lost a hero; Sikhs their chief;
The camp its genius; each and all a friend.
But though our loss struck deeply, what of them?
The widow war-bereft, the orphaned son,
The unseen babe—unseen but not unloved;—
We thought of them; and every man was dumb.

(*The Pioneer*, Allahabad, January 30, 1899.)

APPENDIX C.

AN AMBULANCE RESERVE FOR INDIA.

(From the *Times* of 1st September, 1900.)

TO THE EDITOR OF THE *TIMES*.

SIR,

One of the mainstays, we may even say *the* mainstay, of the Royal Army Medical Corps in South Africa has been the wise measure which the War Office adopted, in sending out from 400 to 500 civilian surgeons, and in utilizing to the full the splendid resources and material placed at its disposal by the British Central Red Cross Committee, which, indeed, has now become an integral part of the War Office. A minor, but none the less valuable, aid to our Army Medical Department has been found in the ambulance services of the colonies. Thanks to all this, the sick and wounded of our Army of 240,000 men have been spared many trials and sufferings which otherwise must have fallen to their lot.

Our great dependency, India, has an army of 70,000 British, 150,000 native, 30,000 volunteer, and 25,000 Imperial Service troops. Of these 100,000, or more, may at any moment be called upon to take the field, while the remainder, left to garrison India, will equally require medical attendance. India at this moment possesses no ambulance reserve whatever. Let South African experiences tell what will be the lot of the sick and wounded of our Indian Army in a possible war with a European Power, and in regions where country and climate and conditions of life are even more unfavourable than on the veldt. It may be argued that, in the event of war, Volunteer ambulance corps, hospitals, and hospital trains would be at once organized. Such impromptu productions would not be one-half as useful as well-regulated establishments which had learned order and method and gained experience by some years of training in peace time. It is precisely those thirty years of training and experience, since the days, in 1870–71, when the Order of St. John of Jerusalem initiated the National Society for the Aid of the Sick and Wounded in War, and when Sir John Furley worked for ten months in the cause of ambulance in France, that has now enabled the British Central Red Cross Committee to give the country an ambulance reserve equivalent to about one-third of the entire medical establishment of the Army in South Africa. So impressed has Professor Chiene, the chief surgeon of the Edinburgh Hospital, been by what he has himself seen in South Africa that he has (in a private letter) recorded his opinion thus—

"The Corps of Civil Surgeons, Army Reserve nurses, and orderlies of the St. John and St. Andrew Ambulance Associations must not be disbanded after the war is over. An Imperial Medical Reserve must be formed to serve her Majesty in future wars. I would aim at a corps of 3000, composed as follows: 1000 doctors (physicians and surgeons), 1000 nurses, 1000 orderlies. To belong to it would be an honour as well as a duty. We must join all these three elements, common to every hospital, together under a Royal corps. If her Gracious Majesty will only say the word it will be done, and well done, too."—*Scotsman*, August 21, 1900.

That is what we want in India—some one, some person of mark and will, to say the word, to give the initiative. For twenty years now isolated efforts have been made at Bombay, Simla, Bangalore, Jaipur, Dalhousie, and doubtless many other places, to establish ambulance instruction and found the nucleus of an ambulance corps. There it has ended. Work dependent on the energy of one or two individuals, whose services may at any time be diverted elsewhere, cannot acquire permanence. Some more stable influence and system is needed. That influence must be sought among those who have authority, and that system must be introduced by those who possess power and command adequate resources. There is in India a very wide field for ambulance work and for the formation of an efficient Ambulance Reserve, which in time of peace will devote itself to the relief of plague, pestilence, famine, sickness, and every form of accident; and in time of war will aid the sick and wounded. This wide field includes, or might include, all Government schools and colleges, municipalities, the police and the Volunteers, manufacturing and mining centres, the States of native chiefs, and the numerous missions, as well as centres and corps maintained in places such as Calcutta, Bombay, Madras, Simla, Poona, Ootacamund, Karachi, Lahore, Rawalpindi, Quetta, Meerut, Delhi, etc., where a more or less considerable number of civilian English people—or, to use the local term, Europeans—reside. The more enlightened natives, ladies and gentlemen, are beginning to take an interest in ambulance work. The Maharajah of Gwalior has given a munificent sum to fit out a hospital ship for China. Native chiefs possess facilities for organizing ambulance transport corps. The medical missionaries, who reside in many native States, are the very men to give ambulance instruction. A knowledge of first aid, nursing, and hygiene is calculated to produce a good effect on the native character. It is a means to an end that the missionary who aims at the education and reform of the native should certainly utilize. The Government of India does not avail itself of the Hindus and Mussulmans in ordinary Volunteer corps. It ought to, and will, do so in Volunteer ambulance corps. In time of war some thousands of trained animals and trained stretcher-bearers are required for the removal of the sick and wounded from the field of battle to the dressing-stations and field hospitals, and thence to the base. A good ambulance system would provide these animals and bearers. Natal sent from 1500 to 2000 bearers to Sir Redvers Buller at Colenso.

Such is the field, such some of the possibilities, for ambulance work in India. Its moral influence on the native cannot fail to be for good. Its practical utility in peace and war is undeniable. We have evidences of that in South Africa. The success of ambulance work in England is largely due to the support, sympathy, and energy of members of our Royal Family, nobility, and gentry. It is earnestly to be hoped that the same support, sympathy, and energy may ere long widen the sphere of its influence and embrace India.

As I bring this letter to a close, the *Times* of Monday (August 20) has reached me, and in it I find the following telegram from Simla, dated August 19—

"Owing to the great demands of the hospitals in connection with the China force, it is probable that all officers of the Indian Medical Service on leave home will be recalled. It is proposed to offer temporary employment to retired officers in the same service. Every effort will be made to equip the hospitals thoroughly, as the autumn is an unhealthy season in North China. The possibility of the plague reviving in India during the cold weather renders the strengthening of the medical service a matter of urgency."

This measure is necessitated when barely 20,000 men are put in the field. What will happen when 100,000 or more are mobilized for service is self-evident.

I am your obedient servant,

A. C. YATE,

Major, Indian Staff Corps.

Culross Park, Culross, N.B., August 21, 1900.

INDEX.

J

K

L

M

N

O

P

R

S

THE END.

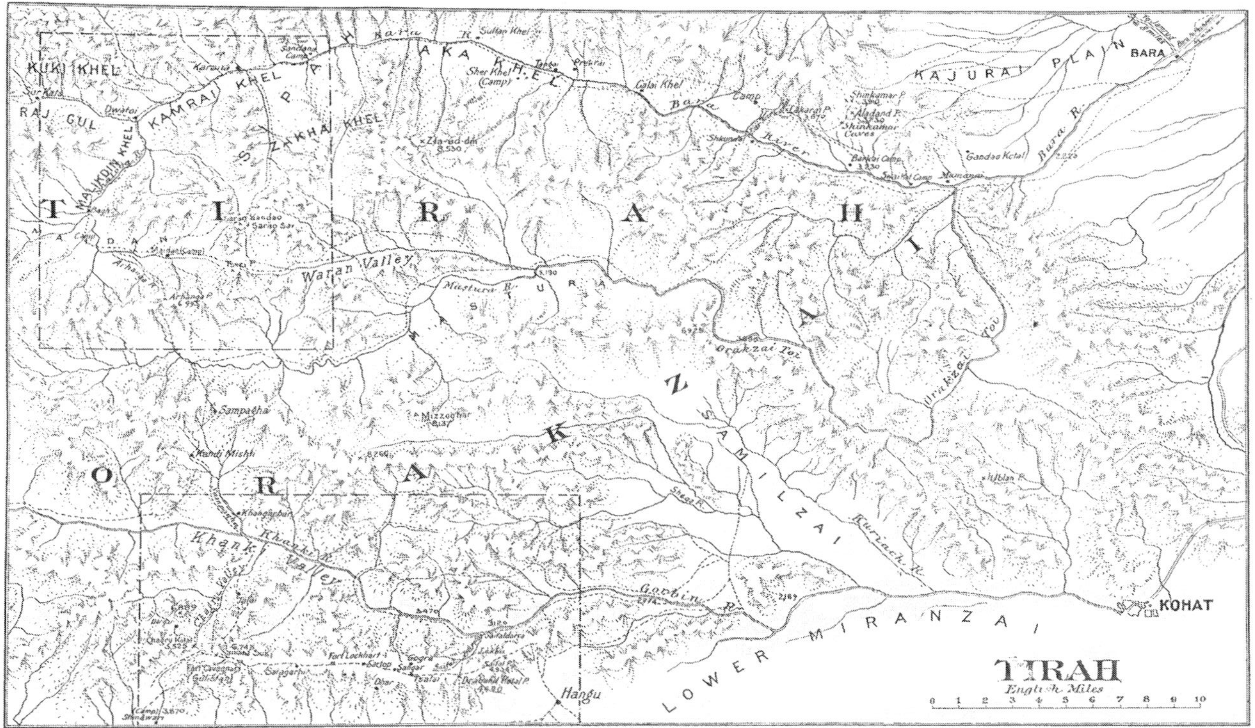
TIRAH
English Miles
0 1 2 3 4 5 6 7 8 9 10
KOHAT
BARA
KAJURAI PLAIN
Bara R.
LOWER MIRANZAI
SAMILZAI
ORAKZAI
TIRAH
Waran Valley
Mastura R.
Khanki R.
Khanki Valley
Kurmach R.
Hangu
Fort Lockhart
KUKI KHEL
RAJ GUL
MALIKDIN KHEL
KAMRAI KHEL
ZAKHA KHEL
AKA KHEL
Sultan Khel
Galai Khel
Sampagha
Mizzeghar
Shinkamar Caves
Gandao Kotal
London: John Murray, Albemarle Street.

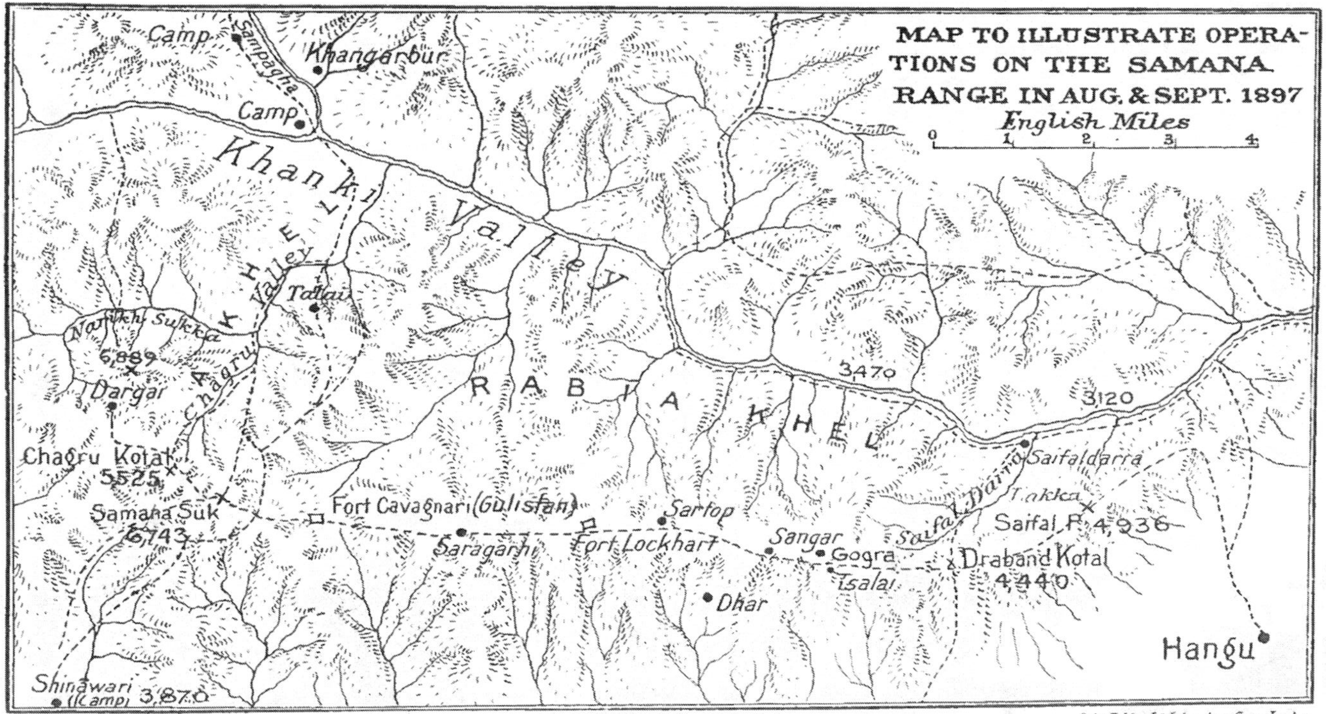

London: John Murray, Albemarle Street.

Gale & Polden Ltd. Lithos, Amen Corner, London.

MAP ILLUSTRATING RECONNAISSAINCES TO SARĀN SAR, THE WARAN VALLEY & DWATOI IN NOV.[R] 1897

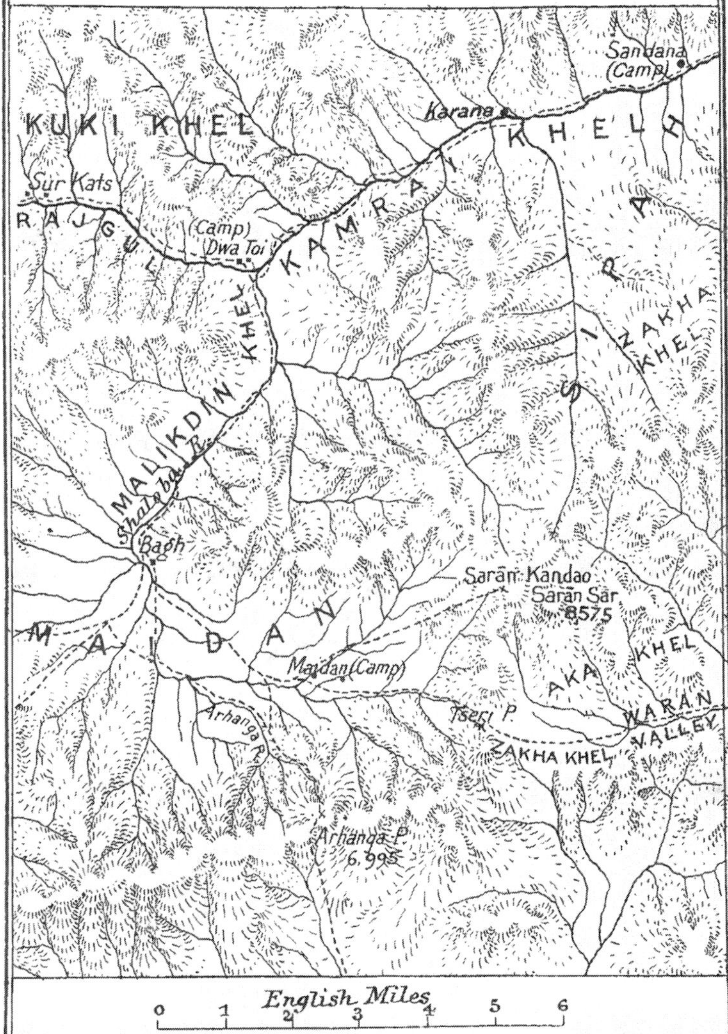